THE
RIDDLE
OF THE
KINGS

A REVELATION OF EVENTS

H.L. MCKNIGHT

THE RIDDLE OF THE KINGS
Copyright © 2020 by Hugh McKnight

ISBN: 978-1-9997955-9-7

Main translations in use: NIV 1978 version
Scripture quotations marked NIV are taken from the holy bible, new international version®, NIV® Copyright © 1973, 1978, 1984, 2011 by Biblica, Inc.® Used by permission. All rights reserved worldwide.

Scripture taken from the Holy Bible, NEW INTERNATIONAL READER'S VERSION® Copyright © 1996, 1998 Biblica. All rights reserved throughout the world. Used by permission of Biblica.

Other translations in use:
Scripture quotations marked NKJV are taken from the New King James Version®. Copyright © 1982 by Thomas Nelson. Used by permission. All rights reserved.

The Revised Standard Version of the Bible, copyright © 1946, 1952, and 1971 the Division of Christian Education of the National Council of the Churches of Christ in the United States of America. Used by permission. All rights reserved.

Emphasis within Scripture quotations is the author's own.

Published by
Maurice Wylie Media
Inspirational Christian Publisher

Publishers' statement: Throughout this book the love for our God is such that whenever we refer to Him we honour with Capitals. On the other hand, when referring to the devil, we refuse to acknowledge him with any honour to the point of violating grammatical rule and withholding capitalisation.

For more information visit
www.MauriceWylieMedia.com

The order of events that will come upon the earth.

'To finish transgression, to put an end to sin, to atone for wickedness, to bring in everlasting righteousness, to seal up vision and prophecy and anoint the most Holy.'
Daniel 9:24

Acknowledgements

In preparing this study, I believe the Holy Spirit led me each step of the way, and at the right time sent me an encourager in Peter who, after reading the work, and at that time ill-prepared and incomplete, gave me the impetus to continue and add to the study, for which I now acknowledge and thank him. And my thanks to Desi for his comments about repetition that pointed the way to restructuring and improving the study, and to David for giving of his valuable time to check for errors. My thanks also go to family members who helped in many various ways. Finally and fully, I want to thank my wife Margaret for her patience and for understanding my need to complete this study, to God's glory.

Endorsement

"Every so often I come across a book that really piques my interest because it pieces together the Scriptures in a way that I haven't been able to do for myself, for various reasons. *The Riddle of the Kings* is one such book. Having had the privilege of sharing ministry and friendship with its author, Lindsay McKnight, I am glad to be able to commend his reverent, prayerful approach to God's Word in allowing it to speak for itself rather than seeking to make it suit a particular theological system or scheme. As the Westminster Confession of Faith says, "when there is a question about the true and full sense of any Scripture… it must be searched and known by other places that speak more clearly". This what this book seeks to do. Lots to think about. Sola Scriptura."

Rev. Peter Dickinson, Muckamore Presbyterian Church, Antrim, Northern Ireland.

"This is an interesting and challenging study of the Book of Revelation which seeks successfully to tie the Apocalyptic Book of the New Testament and the Apocalyptic chapters in the Book of Daniel. The author also investigates tying-in other relevant passages from other Books of the Bible, and an easy-to-understand "The Table of Events" in which he lays out an order in which events prophesied in the Apocalyptic Literature of the Bible will take place."

Rev. George Moore, (Retired Presbyterian Minister)

Contents

Preface

The last book in the Holy Bible is "The Revelation of Jesus Christ" that God gave to show to his servants what must soon take place. He made it known by sending his angel to his servant John, who testifies to everything he saw: that is, the Word of God and the testimony of Jesus. (Revelation1:1–2) The Lord tells the apostle John (Revelation 1:19) to write what he has seen: what is now; a message to the seven churches in the province of Asia. Also (what was to come later) the revelation of His return and the end of the age, on which this study is based. (Revelation chapters 4 -22) Although it is probably not obvious to the reader, what is to come later is about kings and kingdoms that God revealed: not to John, but to the prophet Daniel in dreams. Daniel 11:2-45 is a chronicle of the events that will take place at the time of the end, between the kings of the south and the north. Chapter 7:1-7 reveals four beasts: four kingdoms that will rise from the earth in the last days and be ruled by these kings; and it is by these kings we are able to solve the riddle given to us in Revelation17:9-10 that tests our understanding of what we know about the Revelation.

We begin by putting the events of the Revelation in the order they will occur and present them in the form of a table - The Order of Events. The first seal of the Revelation is opened and the chronicle begins, drawing in events of the Revelation as it proceeds. It is understood by reading across the page from column to column, and events on the same line denoted in highlight are called parallel events in the study.

The table of events is followed by a narrative that puts into words the sequence of events we find in the table. The first two chapters, related by the king of the south and the north each in turn, are a paraphrase of Daniel 11:2-45 that embraces all the events of the revelation …and gives an extra perspective on the vivid visions in his account, from the opening of the first seal and the sequence of catastrophic events that devastate the world before the return of the King of kings. The final chapter of this narrative is allowing Scripture to conclude.

The study begins by setting the scene in heaven (God's Throne, Revelation 4; 5:1-5) and in the hand of Him seated on the throne is a scroll sealed with seven seals. No one worthy is found to open the seals: But a Lamb that looked as if it were slain; He is worthy to open the seals. By Daniel's revelation of the kings and kingdoms, we too are given the key to open the seals by bringing these kings and kingdoms together. We then realise that the first four seals of the Revelation (Revelation 6:1-8) are the four kings and their kingdoms that will appear on earth in the last days. In this, we share with the apostle John the blessing of knowing God's Revelation of what is to come for our world and its people. As the Revelation unfolds, it opens the Scriptures in a way we cannot ignore, and gives place to many of the Old Testament Scriptures. It gives answers, order, and clarity to many questions about the end times that could challenge some long-held beliefs about the Lord's return.

Throughout this study the author endeavours to leave aside all preconceived ideas and let the facts we are given determine the outcome.

This book also contains a supplementary study, "The Feasts of Jehovah" that supports some sections of the Revelation study and gives us a time-line (The Feast of Weeks) from the opening of the first seal to the day of Armageddon. It reveals God's plan for the salvation of the Gentiles, and the foundation on which the sacrament of the Lord's supper stands, and how the redemption of the Jews and the salvation of the Gentiles are entwined.

Introduction

The Book of Revelation brings together some of Man's worst fears: Climate change has become a topic of worldwide concern with its accompanying severe weather. There is likelihood of a catastrophic earthquake along the San Andreas fault, or in the Pacific basin area; perhaps joined with tsunamis. The sooner-or-later impact of a comet or large asteroid has been suggested; the possibility of food and water shortages, and man's selfishness and lust for power provides an underlying uncertainty. It has been the subject of many studies and books; however, I decided that a personal study without the influence of others, and setting aside all my preconceived ideas, would be the most rewarding. I have heard comments about the book of Revelation that suggest it needs to be treated differently from the other scriptures. But why should it not be treated like all the other books of the Bible? Of course, it should be read with the measure of faith given to us, and guided by the Holy Spirit and the Scriptures to an understanding.

What use would it be if the Lord gave us a Revelation we could not understand!
The first three chapters of the Revelation refer to <u>what is now</u>: "The Message to the Churches". I begin at chapter four: <u>what will come later</u>: "The Throne in Heaven". The object of my initial study was to put in order the events of the Revelation as they will occur at the end of the age, and the product is the Table of Events. This sequence of events, I believe, holds the key to a better understanding of this challenging book.

From the outset I realised that the key to open the prophecy was not to be found in the book of Revelation, but in that part of the revelation given to the prophet Daniel. With that came the following insights. First, that Daniel chapter 11 is a chronicle of events that will take place between the kings of the south and north at the end times. These kings rule the four kingdoms, which Daniel in chapter 7 describes as beasts that will rise in the last days. Second, they are the riders of the four horses of the first four seals of the Revelation 6:1-8. As the chronicle progresses, it embraces the unfolding revelation events. When the Lord opens the first seal, the chronicle begins and we begin to understand the Revelation given to the apostle John. We then see what is not immediately obvious from the book of Revelation: that it is about kings and kingdoms, bringing us to the ultimate kingdom, Christ's kingdom on earth, when the saints of the Most High will receive the kingdom for ever and ever. It is by these kings we are able to solve the riddle given to us in Rev.17:9-10 that tests our understanding of what we know about the Revelation.

To help us see what will take place at the end times, I have written an account; the first two chapters by paraphrasing Daniel 11 with events added from the book of Revelation as the revelation unfolds.

The third chapter is composed almost entirely of Scripture. The events of the Revelation, as they occur, are woven into Daniel's chronicle of The Kings of the South and the North. This chronicle of the kings is the foundation and mortar that supports and holds together the events of the revelation as they are revealed from the Scriptures; and is the framework that enables us to reveal all the events in chronological order, until the Lord's coming. These events, and the use of direct text from the New International Bible, are linked in a simple way to tell the story. As it draws to a close with the coming of the King of Kings, the text is almost word for word as they are found in the Scriptures, for after He comes nothing is hidden.

Our story begins with the King of Persia building a kingdom to become the king of the south, and stirring up everyone against the king of the north. The titles, king of the north, and king of the south, are generic, for the titles are passed on as new kings come to power. And it is through the eyes of the king of the south and the king of the north - **each in turn** - we view the unfolding revelation; from the opening of the first seal to the day of Armageddon.

The purpose of the narrative is to put into words the sequence of events we find in the table. This is done without trying to elaborate, or delve in depth into the result of the various events on mankind, or the condition of the earth. The prophet Daniel and the apostle John use great symbolism to describe what they have seen, including the four beasts, but the angel said they were four kingdoms that will rise from the earth. Two comets or asteroids strike the earth, one after the other; no details are given of where in the world they make impact, or what the consequences are for the earth and its people. Some of these events make us aware of the conditions that will exist on earth, and help us to understand why certain things take place, but if we try to unravel the symbolism of the four beasts, or speculate about where the asteroids made impact; where does it lead?

Throughout the study I endeavoured not to use speculation, but let the Scriptures pose the questions and give the answers. In so doing, *it makes alive; and gives place to,* many of the Old Testament Scriptures.

The result is the removal of all preconceived ideas and speculation about what happens when the Lord (Messiah) returns. It gives answers, order, and clarity to many questions about the end times, and these will challenge some long-held beliefs about the Lord's return. It is my prayer that this book will stimulate further study of this portion of God's Word; and strengthen our faith in God who holds our future in His hand.

The supplementary study (The Feasts of Jehovah) supports the sequence of events we find in the table, and confirms the Feast of Weeks as a time-line from the opening of the first seal to the day of Armageddon. It reveals how the redemption of the Jews is entwined with the salvation of the Gentiles.

In Genesis 12, God called Abram to leave his country, the land of Ur of the Chaldeans, and go to the land of Canaan. Ur was in southern Iraq, where our story begins. Abram's journey ended in the promised land, and as we make our way through this study, we too will end our journey in the promised land.

PART ONE
The Revelation Narrative

CHAPTER 1

The Chronicle of the Kings

We cannot ignore Daniel's chronicle about The Kings of the South and the North if we are seeking to understand the Book of Revelation that is based primarily on kings and kingdoms. This chronicle gives an account of the diplomacy and wars between the kingdoms of the North and the South, from the opening of the first of the seven seals of the revelation to the gathering and defeat of the kings of the earth at Armageddon. It places some of the seven seal events in key positions in the Table of Events, including the opening event. It is the framework that embraces all the events of the revelation in chronological order giving continuity to its unfolding; ending with the return of Messiah.

Jesus spoke of kingdoms and nations rising against each other at the end times.

'As he sat on the Mount of Olives, the disciples came to him privately, saying, "Tell us, when will this be, and what will be the sign of your coming and of the close of the age?" And Jesus answered them, "Take heed that no one leads you astray. For many will come in my name, saying, 'I am the Christ,' and they will lead many astray. And you will hear of wars and rumours of wars; see that you are not alarmed; for this must take place, but the end is not yet. For nation will rise against nation, and kingdom against kingdom, and there will be famines and earthquakes in various places: all this is but the beginning of the birth-pangs.' Matthew 24:3-8 RSV

CHAPTER 2

The King of the South

This chapter paraphrases Daniel chapter eleven, with events from The Book of Revelation added as they occur in the unfolding Revelation.

He was a wealthy man, and in the past few years put it to use to become the richest man in Iran, perhaps in the Middle East. The power and control money gave him over people, and the ease it offered to buy friends in the right places, would be the stepping-stones to real power, for he still hungered for something more.

It had taken some time to gain the political power that gave him the absolute control of the nation, and he was proud of all he had achieved. But the lust for power burned deeply within him; fed by the invasion and capture of the countries to the North, South, and west, including Israel, the viper at the bosom of Islam, now with its fangs drawn. Some Israelites claimed their God Jehovah was with them, and would watch over them, but he cared little for them or their god. He alone had given rebirth to the Persian Empire, and he would be the most powerful, sought-after ruler in the world. But now one of his commanders, the leader of his own nation, had become very powerful; it would be a shrewd move on his part if they became allies, for with this commander's full support, greater things could be achieved.

Stirring up anger against the Europeans had not been difficult, for the seeds of resentment and hatred had been well and truly sown over the years. Now they sought to oppose his progress with diplomacy and sanctions, and veiled threats of exclusion, unless there were assurances of how and where his kingdom's resources were traded. The European nations united many years ago, but each retained its own head of state. However, many worldwide pressures, the need for greater political weight, the effect of climate change and scarce resources, forced them to unite under a single head of state. Lately, one known to be a mighty ruler came to power; how and when he chose to ignore them would always be a calculated risk.

The change in climate brought with it more frequent destructive weather events of every kind throughout the world, and over many decades deteriorated to such an extent that lately vast areas of the earth were devastated by hailstorms and lightning. An estimate of a third of the world's vegetation has been destroyed, a third of the grass, and a third of the trees burned up. Populations are on the move in these uninhabitable areas, and the desperate need for food and water has caused riots, looting, and many deaths. Racial hatred has exploded everywhere, with people desperately seeking every means to return to their own countries.

As political pressure increased from the North, he gave more power to his daughter; for she was to succeed him. She shared his analysis of the growing crisis with the North, and agreed with those who advised him on the best course to take; but their advice was not universally accepted by his confidants. Nevertheless, with his daughter and advisers, he went to the king of the North to make an alliance; but the hawks amongst his princes took power and control of the kingdom. Moreover, one of his family declared himself to be king.

The Northern kingdom suffered more than the South from the effect of climate change, and he knew that it would suit the Northerns, at this time, to agree a treaty with this new upstart, as they named him. Now it would not be so easily obtained, for he was convinced by the argument that had brought him to power. He had chosen his time well, for the invasion was a great success, and he plundered the North, taking whatever pleased him. After a time, he decided to leave the king of the North alone and return to his own country, because an asteroid the size of a huge mountain was observed approaching earth's orbit. The astronomers were at a loss to explain why they had failed to raise the alarm earlier, for its trajectory showed that impact with the earth was certain. To allay fear among the people, it was agreed to say it would land in the sea.

His were not the only eyes to observe the growing object in the sky, nor his was the only hope that it would come down in the sea. At first, he felt a great sense of relief as it struck the sea, but after a few days, the first reports indicated massive damage in occupied coastal areas. Soon, reports reached him of the magnitude of the catastrophe: A third of all life in the sea has been killed, and a third of the ships destroyed. Hundreds of thousands lost their lives as great waves swept ashore. Cities, towns and whole communities were left devastated; devoid of any living thing now the water has subsided. Panic quickly spread through the nations as their governments sought ways to deal with the initial problems of drinking water, food, and disease. He was relieved that they had escaped the devastation of the impact, but the worldwide consequences would be a different matter.

For many decades, the possibility of an asteroid strike had been considered likely, and a number of observatories were constantly watching and tracking any that might enter earth's orbit; but comets were not so easy to track, and for the most part unpredictable. The second one was fast approaching the earth, and visible for some time, which indicated its great size: It became a cause of much concern for world leaders, and the scientific community, because its trajectory showed it was certain to strike the earth, with the high probability of a land strike. Where would it fall? What damage will it cause? What new pressures will it bring on the nations? As he considered these questions, reports from intelligence sources raised the alert that a Northern army was on the move. But army commanders thought it most unlikely that an attack would come. However, he ordered the immediate implementation of plans prepared for this event.

Like a great flaming fireball, the comet struck the earth: this time on land. It was many days before communications were sufficiently restored to receive news of the impact, but already there was deterioration of the climate, and he knew it would be across the entire globe. It was like a nuclear winter; debris thrown into the atmosphere blocking out the sunlight; the cold darkness perhaps lasting for a year or more. He knew this would disrupt the food chain and cause widespread environmental damage; but panic was immediate, like a virulent disease that quickly spread throughout the nations. As the situation began to clear, he received reports that estimated a third of the world's rivers were poisoned by the comet. Already many people had died because of the poisoned waters, and some were prepared to kill for safe drinking water and food. Hordes of people were on the move; some supported by armed groups, and people in the areas being overrun were hiding themselves away, trying to protect their families. It was every man for himself at its worst; food and water scarce and costly; hunger and thirst driving men to the depths of despair, leading to the foulest acts of depravity.

It has been a few years since the invasion of the North, and he was sure retaliation would come. They will have been well prepared, having been under great pressure to provide for their people. The invasion came as expected, but his troops were ready, well trained, and deployed according to his plan. The Northerners were easily defeated and forced to retreat. After a few years they raised a large well-equipped army, and once more invaded the South. For a time they had great success and carried the battle deep into the South, but he rallied his forces and counter-attacked; severely beat them, and took many prisoners. He instructed his commanders to show no quarter, and to teach them a lesson; they pursued them and slew thousands. After a time, the order was given to withdraw and return to the South. He was filled with pride, elated at the success of his army that once again had soundly beaten the North. He felt secure, believing his success as a great ruler would be a deterrent to those who thought the resources of the South were to be easily taken.

Although the South, by comparison, was rich in resources; he was concerned for the world's environment; it was getting worse by the day since the asteroids had struck the earth, and now a third of the sun was struck; also a third of the moon; and the stars, so that a third of them turned dark. A third of the day is now without light, and also a third of the night. He was unsure of the cause; perhaps it was cosmic activity yet to be determined; could it be the effects of the "nuclear" winter many lay people favoured? He did not know. Only those who took advantage of every opportunity, every unforgiving moment, would survive in these chaotic times; now was the time to be strong and ruthless. He believed that he alone could save the people from the relentless pressure of the Northerners moving South; had he not already shown them, and those seeking to benefit from his kingdom's wealth, that he could not be beaten. So he encouraged the people to retain some normality to their lives during these most trying and difficult times; this was about to be challenged in a new way.

A great Abyss opened up the ground. Smoke rose from it like the smoke from a gigantic furnace. The sun and sky were darkened by the smoke from the Abyss. Out of the smoke, locusts came down upon the earth, and they were given power like that of scorpions of the earth. They were not allowed to kill men, but could torture them for five months. He suffered, as people world-wide suffered, and the pain endured made him want to die. We cannot begin to imagine what that time was like. The whole world suffered, and almost everything came to a halt until this time of woe was over. Thankfully after five months the excruciating pain ceased, and the sores healed. There was some speculation about the creatures; people said they were demons, from hell itself, for they had human-like faces, and hair like women's hair, and had sharp teeth; their kind had not been seen before. There were a number of men, all Jews, who worship the God of the Israelites, those who said their God was with them; men who had not been with a woman, men who did not lie, and were said to be blameless. Apparently, the creatures could not harm them; giving weight to the theory that they were demons, and those who believed the Christian bible said, "They had a king over them who was called Abaddon in Hebrew, and in Greek Apollyon."

Because the living conditions in the North were so difficult, he knew war would come again, and his intelligence services believed it would be in the next few months. Having beaten them a few times already, it was possible to do it again; but the commanders were alarmed to learn that the Northern army was reported to be 200 million strong. The overwhelming force of the invaders caused him deep concern: even his best troops were unable to stand, and powerless to resist. He ordered them to retreat south, but greater was his alarm to learn that many in his kingdom had assisted the enemy.

The king of the North established himself in the land of Israel that the Jews called the beautiful land, and had the power to destroy it, so he thought it better to wait and see what the Northerners would do next. It was not long before he received an envoy from the king offering him an alliance, and to give him one of his daughters in marriage. He refused to negotiate, and with frustration watched and waited, powerless to take action; his hurt pride fuelling his growing impatience, and anger at being betrayed.

Using the beautiful land as his base, the king of the North turned his attention to the coast lands and took many of them; finally a commander put a stop to his progress, so he returned to the fortress of his own country, where he fell from power, and was no longer to be seen. He waited, hoping it would be possible to negotiate a treaty with the new king which would give more favourable terms, but it was with a sense of foreboding, mixed with impatience, for the North was in political turmoil, and divided into four groups of nations with four heads of state. However, they would act against him as one, for only coming together could they maintain what they had gained from him.

One of the four kings was appointed as tax collector and negotiator, and would not shift from the status quo. After a few years he was destroyed, yet not in anger or in battle; his successor was known to be a contemptible man, who was not given the honour of royalty. He was said to be a master of intrigue, and in a short time, by stealth and deceit, he put down the other three kings, and seized the Northern kingdom. He united it into a more powerful force: a force he had to acknowledge would be difficult to overcome, and most likely refuse his approach for more suitable terms.

CHAPTER 3

The King of the North

This chapter continues to paraphrase Daniel chapter eleven, with events from The Book of Revelation added as they occur in the unfolding Revelation. 2Timothy 3:2 – 5 is also used in the text.

When the master touched him, he was filled with an overwhelming sense of power and authority; felt deep within himself truly destined for the role he was given. He knew it was time to take power, time to rule, time for world domination; success assured in doing the master's will. He was now fully prepared to sacrifice anyone, pay any price, use every means, unashamed to be known as one who made deceit prosper; proud to be known as the master of intrigue.

After the death of the tax-collector, it had not been difficult to discredit the other three kings, and, using every means he could employ, undermined their authority and leadership, and by stealth gained the power to overthrow them. He knew how close he came to failure, for the assassination attempt on his life should have finished him, but the master healed the head wound that should have taken his life. His recovery astonished the whole world, and men followed him, and said, "No one could make war against him." Men worshipped the master, and they worshipped him, because the master had given him his power, his throne, and great authority; and a prophet to help him, who was given power to perform great and miraculous signs, even causing fire to come down from heaven in full view of men.

This power he would use to deceive the inhabitants of the earth into believing he was the god to be worshipped. So he made himself out to be superior; exalted and magnified himself above every god, and said unheard of things against the God of heaven. He encouraged others to do likewise, and inwardly rejoiced as they did.

From the beginning there was dissent and opposition to his very existence, never mind his authority, but he treated it with contempt, something to be dealt with in the near future. He knew there were people who still believed in God, and from the beginning of his rule they spoke out against him. He truly hated them as his master hated them, and looked forward to the time he would wipe them from the face of the earth. But they took courage at this time from two men who claimed to be God's witnesses; they were clothed in sackcloth, a symbolic call for repentance. He knew they were angels who came to earth just before he received power. They were able to strike the earth with every kind of plague; turn water into blood; and had the power to stop it from raining until their time of prophesying was over. But every plague they caused he made it appear that the God of heaven was tormenting the people of the earth, stirring them to anger instead of repentance. Some of those angered tried to kill the angels, but they were destroyed by fire that came from the angel's mouths. The king was confident the master would kill them at a time to suit his purpose.

When he had taken power, he made a covenant of seven years with the richest provinces, captured from the South. He wanted to put them at ease, and assure them of his willingness to continue with the status quo, but he had other plans more suited to his master's will. After a time, when they felt secure, he invaded the South, and swept their armies before him. A prince of the covenant, with whom he had an agreement, was destroyed, for he did not want to be in anybody's debt. From this position of strength, and a kingdom united under his leadership, they would move further south, and control all of the Southern kingdom with its plentiful resources. So he prepared and equipped his army well, with weapons, materials, and purpose. It was an army numerous and strong, ruthless, brutal, and without mercy; an army that would bring the South to its knees and keep it there.

Meanwhile the two angels created great hardship for the people in those areas they chose to cause drought and plagues, and many people were dying from hunger and thirst. Food was scarce and costly with limited choice; water was rationed, and men killed for what they wanted; the deprived died or fought for their needs. This was a time of great woe for the inhabitants of the earth, but a time of opportunity for him. He would soon control the purchase of food and water and every sort of goods; giving him the power to grab hold of the very souls of men, accomplishing the master's desire.

The God of heaven, by sending the two witnesses, wanted men to repent and stop worshipping idols, but he knew they would not. Men had become lovers of themselves, lovers of money, boastful, proud and abusive, disobedient to their parents. He loved how they were, he knew they were ungrateful, unholy, without love, unforgiving, slanderous, without self-control, not lovers of the good. Their treacherous, brutal, conceited nature suited very well his purpose. The master from the very beginning worked in the hearts of men, but now the time to rule on earth was near; time to reap the souls of fallen Man.

About this time, a number of Jews disappeared; taken from the face of the earth. The Christ-lovers were claiming that these were chosen ones redeemed from the earth, and it is written in the scriptures that they will gather to meet with the Lord on Mount Zion, and be presented to the God of Heaven as firstfruits. The master told him their appearance on Mount Zion would be unseen by the people of the earth, and would encourage the Christians, to no avail. As for the rest of mankind, the disappearance of Jews from the face of the earth would easily be forgotten. He recalled the time the master released the demons from the abyss to inflict sores on men for five months; there were men whom the demons could not hurt. The master said these were the same men, 144,000 Jews, and it mattered little: for soon he would have absolute power to rule the world.

After this, an angel flying in mid-air proclaimed the eternal gospel to every nation, tribe, language, and people who live on the earth. He said in a loud voice, "Fear God and give him the glory, because the hour of His judgement had come." He also said, "worship Him who made the heavens, the earth, the sea, and the springs of water."

Men had been conditioned over many years, and by numerous means, to accept the presence of demons and angels, just like the two who were causing such havoc with their drought and plagues. The appearance of this angel raised no alarm, and the king was deeply gratified to know that the gospel fell mostly on deaf ears. So he encouraged the worship of demons all the more, and cursed and blasphemed the angels and the God of heaven, saying unheard-of things against them, and showed his favour to men who did likewise.

He could wait no longer to invade the South. The army was well equipped, trained, and honed to readiness for war. His destiny of world rule and the domination and enslavement of men everywhere to the master's will now began. The Southern king had raised a large powerful army, but was unable to stand against him because of the plots he had devised, because a few well-placed spies within the Southern King's close followers ensured his deceit would prosper. So they swept the armies of the South before them and slew thousands, killing without mercy.

In the days following the war, a second angel appeared. His message foretold the destruction of Babylon the Great, who had become a source of nuisance to him; this prophecy he thought to fulfil. The angel said. "Fallen! Fallen is Babylon the Great, which made all the nations drink the maddening wine of her adulteries." He hated this Babylon, who was under a powerful delusion claiming to represent Christ on earth that gave her authority over many peoples and nations. She had served the master well for decades, leading men astray by telling them they could have salvation; a place in heaven through her teachings and the communion of her cup. He knew her end would come, and it would be by his hand even though an angel proclaimed it.

The king of the South raised another large army that was easily defeated. His troops lacked their former courage and were unable to stand against him. He established his base in the so-called Beautiful Land, where he met the king of the South when he sued for peace, and agreed to sit with him at the same table to discuss terms and conditions; having no intention of giving up anything gained, but further to deceive him. He knew the king of the South was lying, but to no purpose; he himself was the master of deceit.

He plundered the South and returned to his own country taking with him great wealth, but his heart was set against the Holy Covenant. He ordered his commanders to take coercive action against them, and reward those who violated the covenant they had with their God. When the time was right, he ordered the army to invade further South, but was opposed by ships of the western coast lands. He turned back, and again poured out his fury against the Holy Covenant, and as before those who forsook it were to be shown great favour and to receive great reward.

As he sought to bring an end to those who testified to the Word of God, and those who held fast to the Holy Covenant, a third angel flew in mid-air, and with a loud voice he shouted "If anyone worships the beast or his image and receives his mark on the forehead or on the hand, he too will drink the wine of God's fury, which has been poured full strength into the cup of His wrath. He will be tormented with burning sulphur in the presence of the holy angels and of the Lamb; and the smoke of their torment rises for ever and ever. There is no rest day or night for those who worship the beast and his image, or for anyone who receives the mark of his name." He knew this would be a call for endurance on part of those who obey God's commandments and remained faithful to Christ, but what he had in mind for them would test them and their faith to the utmost. And this, like all the other heavenly messages, would fall on the deaf ears of the others; if it did penetrate their wayward minds it would soon be gone.

Now was the time to fulfil satan's will, for his time to rule on earth was at hand. He ordered his armed forces to desecrate the temple fortress of the Jews, and abolish the daily sacrifice to their God. Claiming to be as great as the Prince of Hosts, the prophet set up an image of him in the temple that was given power to speak. Everyone was to worship it. Those who did not worship his image were to be put to death. The prophet ordered people everywhere to receive the number of the master's name as a mark on their forehead or right hand, for the time had come to control the purchase of food and water and every sort of goods. He forced this upon them, for no one could buy or sell unless they had the mark. He knew they would pay little heed to the angel's warning; hunger and thirst were compelling motivators. So everyone who received the mark of the beast rebelled against the God of heaven.

However, the angel's warning encouraged and assured the Christians, even as they were put to death by the sword, or burned, they quoted Revelation 14:13, *'Blessed are the dead who die in the Lord from now on. Yes, says the Spirit, they will rest from their labour, for their deeds will follow them.'*

They said it was written for their time. He tested their assurance and faithfulness with death.

The master's time to rule on earth came at last. Claiming to be God, he set himself up in the temple of the Jews, for all power and authority on earth were his. He destroyed the city he knew the God of heaven loved, and men everywhere worshipped him. Those who knew their God, those who bore witness to Christ and the word of God, firmly resisted the master, but he prospered in everything, and truth was thrown to the ground. He trampled the host of the saints underfoot to show his contempt for their God, and encouraged all who violated the covenant they had with the God of heaven, and by flattery he corrupted many, but the Christians said, "satan's power and authority over the world was the third woe, foretold in the book of Revelation." It mattered little to the king, for they were all put to death.

The two witnesses who had caused so much hardship by their plagues and drought were in Jerusalem, their testimony at an end. They had been a source of annoyance to him for the past three and a half years, but now came face to face with the master. The master attacked them, overpowered, and killed them; their bodies lay in the street of the great city, which is figuratively called Sodom and Egypt, where also their Lord was crucified. For three and a half days, men from every people, tribe and language, gazed on their bodies and refused them burial. They gloated over them and celebrated by sending each other gifts, because the prophets had tormented those who lived on the earth. But after three and a half days a breath of life entered their bodies, they stood on their feet, and terror struck those who saw them. Those standing around the scene heard a loud voice, some said the voice of God, which said, *"Come up here."* And they went up to Heaven in a cloud, as they looked on, it was then satan said we were to claim this event as a defeat of the God of Heaven, for it looked as if they were removed out of his reach. And men gave their allegiance to the master, and worshipped him because of his presence and authority on earth.

Now that the power of the Holy Ones was finally broken, and the daily sacrifice and the host of the saints given over to him; he knew the God of heaven would vent His wrath against all creation. And so it began, with ugly painful sores on those who bore satan's mark, and

CHAPTER 4

The King of Kings and Lord of Lords

'The satanic forces gathered at Armageddon to wait for the ten kings of the earth to join with them in battle against the King of kings and the Lord of lords. But God's wrath continued; the Earth dries up and withers, the world languishes and withers, the exalted of the earth languish. The earth is defiled by its people, they had disobeyed the laws, violated the statues and broke the everlasting covenant. Therefore, a curse consumes the earth; its people must bear their guilt. Therefore, earth's inhabitants are burned up, and very few are left.' Isaiah 24:4-6

Then... *'There was a great earthquake. The sun turned black like sackcloth made of goat hair, the whole moon turned blood red, and the stars in the sky fell to earth, as late figs drop from a fig tree when shaken by a strong wind. The sky receded like a scroll, rolling up, and every mountain and island was removed from its place. - No earthquake like it has ever occurred since man has been on earth, so tremendous was the quake. The great city split into three parts, and the cities of the nations collapsed. God remembered Babylon the Great and gave her the cup filled with the wine of the fury of his wrath. Every island fled away and the mountains could not be found. From the sky huge hailstones of about a hundred pounds each fell upon men. And they cursed God on account of the plague of hail, because the plague was so terrible.'* Revelation 6:12-14; 16:18-21

For... *'The flood gates of the heavens are opened, the foundations of the earth shake. The earth is broken up, the earth is split asunder, the earth is thoroughly shaken. The earth reels like a drunkard, it sways like a hut in the wind, so heavy upon it is the guilt of its rebellion that it falls - never to rise again.'* Isaiah 24:18-20

And it was at this time... *'God remembered Babylon the Great and gave her the cup filled with the wine of the fury of his wrath.'* Revelation 16:19

And God knows... *'The beast and the ten horns will hate the prostitute. They will bring her to ruin and leave her naked; they will eat her flesh and burn her with fire. For God has put it into their hearts to accomplish his purpose by agreeing to give the beast their power to rule, until God's words are fulfilled and He gave her the cup filled with the wine of fury of his wrath.'* Revelation 17:16-18

'After this I heard what sounded like the roar of a great multitude in heaven shouting: "Hallelujah! Salvation and glory and power belong to our God, for true and just are His judgements. He has condemned the great prostitute who corrupted the earth with her adulteries. He has avenged on her the blood of His servants." And again they shouted: "Hallelujah! The smoke of her goes up for ever and ever." Revelation 19:1 "Amen, Hallelujah."

The Amen is given to the destruction of Babylon the Great, the Mother of Prostitutes, and to the end of God's wrath against a fallen rebellious world; and the Heavens opened and the sign of the Son of Man appeared in the sky.

'And I saw heaven standing open and there before me was a white horse, whose rider is called Faithful and True. With justice He judges and makes war. His eyes are like blazing fire, and on his head are many crowns. He has a name written on him that no one knows but he himself. He is dressed in a robe dipped in blood, and His name is The Word of God. On His robe and on His thigh He has this name written: King of Kings and Lord of Lords. The armies of Heaven follow Him, riding on white

horses and dressed in fine linen, white and clean. Out of his mouth comes
a sharp sword with which to strike down the nations. "He will rule them
with an iron sceptre." He treads the wine press of the fury of the wrath of
God Almighty. On his robe and on his thigh he has this name written:

"KING OF KINGS AND LORD OF LORDS."
Revelation 19:11-16

'Then I saw the beast and the kings of the earth and their armies gathered
together to make war against the rider on the horse and his army. But the
beast was captured and with him the false prophet who had performed
the miraculous signs on his behalf. With these signs he had deluded those
who had received the mark of the beast and worshipped his image. The
two of them were thrown alive into the fiery lake of burning sulphur. The
rest of them were killed with the sword that came out of the mouth of the
rider on the white horse.' Revelation 19:19-21

'On that day His feet will stand on the Mount of Olives, east of Jerusalem,
and the Mount of Olives will be split in two from east to west, forming
a great valley, with half of the mountain moving north and half moving
south -This is the plague with which the Lord struck all the nations that
fought against Jerusalem: Their flesh will rot while they are still standing
on their feet, their eyes will rot in their sockets, and their tongues will rot
in their mouths. On that day men will be stricken by the Lord with great
panic. Each man will seize the hand of another, and they will attack each
other.' Zechariah 14:4, 12-13

'And I saw an angel coming down out of heaven, having the key to the Abyss
and holding in his hand a great chain. He seized the dragon that ancient
serpent, who is the devil, or satan, and bound him for a thousand years. He
threw him into the Abyss, and locked and sealed it over him, to keep him
from deceiving the nations any more until the thousand years were ended.
After that, he must be set free for a short time.' Revelation 20:1-3

'And I (the Lord) will pour out on the House of David and of the inhabitants of Jerusalem, a spirit of grace and supplication. They will look on me the one they have pierced, and they will mourn for Him as one mourns for an only child, and grieved bitterly for Him as one grieves for a first born son.' Zechariah 12:10

Messiah, who their forefathers rejected, has come.
'Lord and king over the whole earth. On that day there will be one Lord, and His name the only name.' Zechariah 14:9

'Shout and be glad, O Daughter of Zion. For I am coming, and will live among you" declares the Lord. "Many nations will be joined with the Lord in that day and will become my people. I will live among you and you will know how the Lord Almighty has sent me to you.' Zechariah 2:10-11

Then... *'I saw thrones on which were seated those who were given authority to judge. And I saw the souls of those who were beheaded because of their testimony for Jesus and because of the word of God. They had not worshipped the beast or his image and had not received his mark on their foreheads or their hands. They came to life and reigned with Christ a thousand years. (The rest of the dead did not come alive until the thousand years were ended.) This is the first resurrection. Blessed and holy are those who have part in the first resurrection. The second death has no power over them, but they will be priests of God and of Christ and will reign with him for a thousand years.'* Revelation 20:4-6

'In the last days the mountain of the Lord's temple will be established as chief among the mountains; it will be raised above the hills, and all the nations will stream to it. Many peoples will come and say, "Come let us go up to the mountain of the Lord, to the house of the God of Jacob. He will teach us his ways, so that we may walk in his paths."

The law will go out from Zion, the word of the Lord from Jerusalem. He will judge between the nations and will settle disputes for many peoples.

PART TWO

The Revelation of Events Study

CHAPTER 5

The First Seal | The Scroll

This study is not a commentary on the Book of Revelation, but it gives us an understanding of it by putting the events in the order they will occur. This was the ground-work of my study. It was made possible by learning that God gave Daniel the key to open the Revelation. It was revealed to Daniel that four kingdoms will rise from the earth in the last days, but the saints of the Most High will receive the kingdom and will possess it for ever and ever. And kingdoms have kings, of whom Daniel gives a chronological account under the heading of the kings of the South and North. And with the realisation that the horse riders of the first four seals of the revelation are kings of the four kingdoms, we can open the first four seals. As I have already stated, this chronicle of the kings embraces all the events of the Revelation from the opening of the first seal to the gathering of the kings at Armageddon.

As we begin our study. I want first of all to set the scene in heaven.

The Throne in Heaven

After this I looked, and there before me was a door standing open in heaven. And the voice I had first heard speaking to me like a trumpet said, "Come up here, and I will show you what must take place after this." At once I was in the Spirit, and there before me was a throne in heaven with someone sitting on it. And the one who sat there had the appearance of jasper and carnelian. A rainbow, resembling an emerald, encircled the throne. Surrounding the throne were twenty-four other

*thrones, and seated on them were twenty four elders. They were dressed
in white and had crowns of gold on their heads. From the throne came
flashes of lightning, rumblings and peals of thunder. Before the throne,
seven lamps were blazing. These are the seven spirits of God. Also before
the throne there was what looked like a sea of glass, clear as crystal. In
the centre, around the throne, were four living creatures, and they were
covered with eyes, in front and in back. The first living creature was like a
lion, the second was like an ox, the third had a face like a man, the fourth
was like a flying eagle. Each of the four living creatures had six wings and
was covered with eyes all around, even under his wings. Day and night
they never stop saying. "Holy, holy, holy is the Lord God Almighty, who
was, and is to come." Whenever the living creatures give glory, honour
and thanks to him who sits on the throne and who lives for ever and ever,
the twenty-four elders fall down before him who sits on the throne, and
worship him who lives for ever and ever. They lay their crowns before the
throne and say: "You are worthy, our Lord and God, to receive glory and
honour and power, for you created all things, and by your will they were
created and have their being.'* Revelation 4:1-11*

*'Then I saw in the right hand of him who sat on the throne a scroll with
writing on both sides and sealed with seven seals. And I saw a mighty
angel proclaiming in a loud voice," Who is worthy to break the seals and
open the scroll?" But no one in heaven or on earth or under the earth could
open the scroll or even look inside it. I wept and wept because no one was
found who was worthy to open the scroll or look inside. Then one of the
elders said to me, "Do not weep! See the Lion of the tribe of Judah, the
root of David, has triumphed. He is able to open the scroll and its seven
seals." Then I saw a Lamb, looking as if it had been slain, standing in the
centre of the throne, encircled by the four living creatures and the elders.
He had seven horns and seven eyes, which are the seven spirits of God sent
out into the whole earth. He came and took the scroll from the right hand
of him who sat on the throne. And when he had taken it, the four living
creatures and the twenty four elders fell down before the Lamb. Each one
had a harp and they were holding golden bowls full of incense, which are*

For the events to begin, the first seal must be opened. So what is the opening event?

There are two main apocalyptic books in the Bible, notwithstanding many other sections of scripture elsewhere in the Bible. But it is from the book of Daniel that the Lord shows us the way to unlock the seals of the Revelation. Long before the book of Revelation was given to the apostle John, the Lord forged the key: gave us the apocalyptic chapters of Daniel to be part of the revelation. That being so, we have one revelation from these two books of the Bible, and we treat those chapters of Daniel as text in the book of Revelation. So that, when the Lord opens the first seal, the chronicle of the king of the South and the North begins, and from it we identify the king on the white horse called forth by the Lord; also his kingdom, the first to rise from the earth.

Daniel's chronicle of the kings of the South and the North embraces all the events of the revelation, and it is to this we turn to guide our thoughts. At present, I see no reason to unravel the symbolism that Daniel uses to describe the four beasts in his dream. In the angel's interpretation, he is simply told they are four kingdoms. As far as I understand, the symbolism used throughout the revelation by the apostle John and the prophet Daniel is like a cloak that covers the underlying straightforward story of the revelation. That is not to say it has no value, or would not enrich and add to our study. Our purpose is to place the events in the order they occur, but first discover the opening event.

The Lamb opens the first seal: Daniel's chronicle of the kings begins

'I watched as the Lamb opened the first of the seven seals. Then I heard one of the four living creatures say in a voice like thunder, "Come!" I looked, and there before me was a white horse! Its rider held a bow, and he was given a crown, and he rode out as a conqueror bent on conquest.'
Revelation 6:1-2

A king is brought forth, and given a crown; so also a kingdom

The first kingdom to rise from the earth
'*The first beast was like a lion, and it had wings of an eagle. I watched until its wings were torn off and it was lifted from the ground so that it stood on two feet like a man, and the heart of a man was given to it.*' Daniel 7:4

Kingdoms have kings
At the heart of the beast - the kingdom - is a man: a king. Kingdoms have kings! But who is the King? Where is his kingdom?

When the first seal is opened, Daniel's vision of a ram and a goat begins to be fulfilled.
'*In my vision I saw myself in the citadel of Susa in the province of Elam; in the vision I was beside the Ulai Canal. I looked up and there before me was a ram with two horns standing beside the canal, and the horns were long. One of the horns was longer than the other but grew up later. I watched the ram as he charged toward the west and the north and the south. No one could stand against him, and none could rescue from his power. He did as he pleased and became great.*' Daniel 8:2-4

Daniel is given the meaning of the vision
'*The angel said "I am going to tell you what will happen later in the time of wrath, because the vision concerns the appointed time of the end. The two horned ram you saw represents the kings of Media and Persia.*' Daniel 8:19-20

We are left in no doubt that this is an end-time event, but does this rider on the white horse, the two-horned ram, represent the kings of Media and Persia?

'*Now then I tell you the truth: three more kings will appear in Persia, and then a fourth, who will be far richer than all the others. When he*

has gained power by his wealth, he will stir up everyone against the kingdom of Greece. The king of the South will become strong, but one of his commanders will become even stronger than he and will rule his own kingdom with great power. After some years they will become allies.'
Daniel 11:2,5-6a

The southern kingdom exists by someone coming to power in Persia; forming an alliance with the king of Media; conquering countries to the west, the north, and the south including Israel, to become the king of the South. This kingdom must be established; the king of the South must become great before he stirs up everyone against the kingdom of Greece. Here the lines are drawn in a north-south divide by this king and kingdom; brought into existence when the Lord commands the first seal to be opened, so that other events can take place. The wars between the North and South result finally in the domination of the northern king, who plays a key part in revealing the man of lawlessness. He, according to Paul, must be revealed before the King of Kings and the Lord of Lords comes to reign.

The first seal is opened.
The rider on the white horse - the king of Persia rides out.
The first seal: The rider held a bow, was given a crown and rode out as a conqueror bent on conquest.
The ram with two horns: He charged toward the west and the north and the south. No one could stand against him.
The king of Persia becomes the king of the South.

The first stone has been thrown; we need to see how many times it struck the water.
'After this I saw four angels standing at the four corners of the earth, holding back the four winds of the earth to prevent any wind from blowing on the land or on the sea or on any tree. Then I saw another angel coming up from the east, having the seal of God. He called out in a loud voice to the four angels who had been given power to harm the

land and the sea: "Do not harm the land or the sea or the trees until we
put a seal on the foreheads of the servants of our God." Then I heard
the number of those who were sealed. 144,000 from the twelve tribes of
Israel.' Revelation 7:1-4

In Revelation chapter 6 we are given the first six seals followed by this
act of God but that does not mean it finds its place with or after the
sixth seal event, as John says at the beginning of chapter seven. "After
this I saw" After what? After the Lord had shown him the events of
the six seals. This is the first event to take place after the first seal is
opened. God puts his seal (as with Cain in Genesis 4:15) on 144,000
men from the twelve tribes of Israel. They are under God's protection
until their purpose is revealed, and this period must include the time
the southern kingdom is established when the king of the South
captures the nations around him including Israel. After this act of
God, the four angels holding back the four winds of the earth make
way for an angel to sound the first trumpet.

'The first angel sounded his trumpet, and there came hail and fire mixed
with blood, and it was hurled down upon the earth. A third of the earth
was burned up a third of the trees were burned up, and all the green grass
was burned up.' Revelation 8:7

We do not know precisely when the first trumpet event took place but
we can say that, about this time, a third of the earth, a third of the
trees, and all the green grass were burned up. We can also imagine the
effect this will have upon the inhabitants of the earth, even though
we do not know where it took place. We do not know for sure what
comes next, but we can get help to make a decision by reference to
our framework passage.

'Now I tell you the truth: Three more kings will appear in Persia, and
then a fourth, who will be far richer than all the others. When he has
gained power by his wealth, he will stir up everyone against the kingdom

of Greece. Then a mighty king will appear, who will rule with great power and do as he pleases. After he has appeared, his empire will be broken up and parcelled out to the four winds of heaven.' It will not go to his descendants, nor will it have the power he exercised, because his empire will be uprooted and given to others. Daniel 11:2-4

The time between the king of the South's gaining power and the appearance of the mighty king is a short period of time. So it is reasonable to assume there was only one trumpet event after the first seal was opened.

The first seal is opened - The Feast of Weeks and the Chronicle of the Kings begins.

God puts a seal on the forehead of 144,000 Jews.

The king of Persia rides forth as a conqueror to become the king of the South.

An angel sounds the first trumpet: A third of the earth, a third of the trees, and all the green grass were burned up.

Time to open the second seal.

CHAPTER 6

The Second Seal | The First Woe

'I, Daniel, was troubled in spirit, and the visions that passed through my mind disturbed me. I approached one of those standing there and asked him the true meaning of all this. "So he told me the interpretation of these things: 'the four great beasts are four kingdoms that will rise from the earth. But the saints of the Most High will receive the kingdom and will possess it forever - yes, for ever and ever.' Daniel 7:15-18

Having raised the first of the four kingdoms and its king, we could assume the rider on the horse of the second seal is also one of the kings. Indeed, we could make that assumption about this one and the next two. The first four seals represent the kings of the four kingdoms that will rise from the earth. Nevertheless, we need to justify that assumption.

The Lord opens the second seal; the mighty king rides out
'When the Lamb opened the second seal, I heard the second living creature say, "Come!" Then another horse came out, a fiery red one. Its rider was given power to take peace from the earth and to make men slay each other. To him was given a large sword.' Revelation 6:3-4

The second kingdom
'The second beast looked like a bear. It was raised up on one of its sides, and it had three ribs in its mouth between its teeth. It was told, "get up and eat your fill of flesh!" Daniel 7:5

The rider of the fiery red horse is given a large sword, and the power to take peace from the earth and make men slay one another. The beast is told, "get up and eat your fill of flesh." To put it another way, "make men slay one another" with the means to do it: the large sword. Perhaps we could say that this rider is the king of the second kingdom, but without conviction. This king is given power to take peace from the earth, and make men slay one another. To do that he would at least need a power base. To have the ability to make his influence worldwide, it would need to be a kingdom, and a powerful one at that: a kingdom that already existed before the king of Persia became the king of the South.

Can our key passage help us to identify the second king?
'Now I tell you the truth: Three more kings will appear in Persia, and then a fourth, who will be far richer than all the others. When he has gained power by his wealth, he will stir up everyone against the kingdom of Greece. Then a mighty king will appear, who will rule with great power and do as he pleases. After he has appeared, his empire will be broken up and parcelled out to the four winds of heaven.' Daniel 11:2-4

Then a mighty king will appear
This mighty king is called forth by the second seal event; he comes to power just after the king of the south is established, and is the latest of a line of kings of the northern kingdom: the kingdom of Greece. As we follow this line of northern kings, we will see his kingdom, his empire, divided: parcelled out to the four winds of heaven. But first, the king of the South, when he has gained power by his great wealth, stirs up everyone against the kingdom of Greece.

We need to bring the king of Greece unto the scene to allow this to happen
'As I was thinking about this, suddenly a goat with a prominent horn between his eyes came from the west, crossing the whole earth without touching the ground. He came toward the two-horned ram I had seen

standing beside the canal and charged at him in great rage. I saw him attack the ram furiously, striking the ram and shattering his two horns. The ram was powerless to stand against him, the goat knocked him to the ground and trampled on him, and none could rescue the ram from his power; the goat became very great.' Daniel 8:5-8

Daniel is given the interpretation
'The two-horned ram you saw represents the kings of Media and Persia. The shaggy goat is the king of Greece, the large horn between his eyes is the first king.' Daniel 8:20-21

I do not believe we are to think there was a Grecian Empire, but a European state that existed prior to the southern kingdom being formed. Perhaps ruled by a Greek king, or simply because Greece is the nearest part of Europe to the southern kingdom. Greece is due north of Turkey and the middle eastern area. However, in the Scripture the shaggy goat with a prominent horn between his eyes came from the west. From the north and from the west implies Western Europe, and could include part or all of central Europe. The prominent horn suggests other "lesser" rulers in the makeup of the kingdom. When Daniel calls this kingdom an empire he is prophesying about the rise of the Roman Empire again. (Rev.17:7-8) This is the mighty king who will rule with great power, and do as he pleases. In Daniel's chronicle of the kings, he follows immediately after the king of Persia. We need this king of Greece to allow these things to happen: the north-south divide, the diplomacy, the ensuing wars and their outcomes, until the time of wrath is complete.

The second seal is opened. The mighty king of Greece, king of the North, rides forth.

The second trumpet calls forth its event
'The second angel sounded his trumpet, and something like a huge mountain, all ablaze, was thrown into the sea. A third of the sea turned

into blood, a third of the living creatures in the sea died, and a third of the ships were destroyed.' Revelation 8:8-9

As before, we are not told where this event occurred, or what the consequence would be for the earth and its people. We can only speculate; it would be a catastrophe for mankind. We also need to know if this was the only event to follow the second seal. In reference to our framework passage there is nothing we can draw on to help, that is, until we come to the sixth trumpet event that provides a link.

'The third angel sounded his trumpet, and a great star, blazing like a torch, fell from the sky on a third of the rivers and on the springs of water - the name of the star is Wormwood. A third of the waters turned bitter, and many people died from the waters that had become bitter. The fourth angel sounded his trumpet, and a third of the sun was struck, and a third of the moon, and a third of the stars, so that a third of them turned dark. A third of the day was without light and also a third of the night. As I watched, I heard an eagle that was flying in mid-air call out in a loud voice: "Woe! Woe! Woe! to the inhabitants of the earth, because of the trumpet blasts about to be sounded by the other three angels.' Revelation 8:10-13

We are not given locations for the comet or asteroid strikes. However, we can say that the first four trumpet events would have devastated the whole world. We can also understand something of the effect on the environment; creating conditions that cause population shifts; the scarcity of food and water, and the outbreak of diseases. Conditions like this would make necessary the control of people and scarce resources, leading to inevitable disputes and wars.

The last three trumpets have within them three events that herald a time of woe for the earth. I have treated the woe events to a separate column in the table, because our attention is directed to them, and to note their special place in the order of events. There are various references to the time of woe in the bible and there is the natural assumption that this time of woe is a continuous period. But Revelation 9:12 tells us that the first woe is past; two other woes are yet to come.

The first of the woes comes as a single event of the fifth trumpet

'The fifth angel sounded his trumpet, and I saw a star that had fallen from the sky to the earth. The star was given the key to the shaft of the Abyss. When he opened the Abyss, smoke rose from it like the smoke from a gigantic furnace. The sun and sky were darkened by the smoke from the Abyss. And out of the smoke locusts came down upon the earth and were given power like that of scorpions of the earth. They were told not to harm the grass of the earth or any plant or tree, but only those people who did not have the seal of God on their foreheads. They were not given power to kill them, but only to torture them for five months. And the agony they suffered was like that of the sting of a scorpion when it strikes a man. During those days men will seek death, but will not find it; they will long to die, but death will elude them. The locusts looked like horses prepared for battle. On their heads they wore something like crowns of gold, and their faces resembled human faces. Their hair was like woman's hair, and their teeth were like lion's teeth. They had breastplates like breastplates of iron, and the sound of their wings was like the thundering of many horses and chariots rushing into battle. They had tails and stings like scorpions, and in their tails they had power to torment people for five months. They had as king over them the angel of the Abyss, whose name in Hebrew is Abaddon, and in Greek, Apollyon. The first woe is past; two other woes are yet to come.' Revelation 9:1-12

More power is given to satan on the earth

The key to the shaft of the Abyss was given to satan. He was permitted to open it and release demons that were limited in what they were allowed to do. The satanic forces were still held back by the continuing presence of the Holy Spirit on earth. From this we can see that satan's time has not yet come. Christians living at this time suffer the sores

CHAPTER 7

The Third Seal | The Little Scroll

The third seal

'When the Lamb opened the third seal, I heard the third living creature say, "Come!" I looked, and there before me was a black horse! Its rider was holding a pair of scales in his hand. Then I heard what sounded like a voice among the four living creatures, saying, "A quart of wheat for a day's wage, and three quarts of barley for a day's wage, and do not damage the oil and the wine!" Revelation 6:5

The third beast

'After that, I looked, and there before me was another beast, one that looked like a leopard. And on its back it had four wings like those of a bird. This beast had four heads, and it was given authority to rule.' Daniel 7:6

This beast with four heads has only one rider who is given no great task to perform, no kingdom building, no slaying of thousands, but given authority to rule on behalf of the four heads.

We need to see if our key passage will help

'Now then I tell you the truth: Three more kings will appear in Persia. And then a fourth, who will be far richer than all the others. When he has gained power by his wealth, he will stir up everyone against the kingdom of Greece. Then a mighty king will appear, who will rule with great power and do as he pleases. After he has appeared, his empire will be broken up and parcelled out toward the four winds of Heaven. It will not go to his

descendants, nor will it have the power he exercised, because his empire will be up-rooted and given to others.' Daniel 11:2-4

Here is the rise to power of the king of Persia who becomes the king of south. Then a mighty king comes to power, a king of the North, the rider on the fiery red horse of the second seal, whose empire is divided into four: "parcelled out toward the four winds of heaven."

This mighty king of the North invades the south

'He will establish himself in the beautiful land and will have the power to destroy it. He will determine to come with the might of his entire kingdom, and will make an alliance with the king of the South. And he will give him a daughter in marriage, in order to overthrow the kingdom, but his plan will not succeed or help him. Then he will turn his attention to the coast lands and will take many of them, but a commander will put an end to his insolence and will turn his insolence back upon him. After this, he will turn back toward the fortress of his own country but will stumble and fall, to be seen no more.' Daniel 11:16-19

In verse 20

'His successor will send out a tax collector to maintain the royal splendour. In a few years however, he will be destroyed, yet not in anger or in battle.'

We have this rider on a black horse with a pair of scales in his hand; the representative king of the divided Northern kingdom. A tax collector, given authority to rule for a few years, then destroyed, but not in anger or in battle. Perhaps these words suggest divine intervention. (The Lord opens the fourth seal.) The four kingdoms of the divided northern kingdom are treated as one beast by the Lord, because it is the whole northern kingdom he brings against the south. However, three other kings rule in their kingdoms.

The rider on the black horse, the king of Daniel's third beast with four heads, rides out.

The third stone has been thrown - What happens next?

'Then I saw another mighty angel coming down from heaven. He was robed in a cloud, with a rainbow above his head; his face was like the sun, and his legs were like fiery pillars. He was holding a little scroll in his hand. He planted his right foot on the sea and his left foot on the land, and he gave a loud shout like the roar of a lion. When he shouted, the voices of the seven thunders spoke. And when the seven thunders spoke, I was about to write; but I heard a voice from heaven say, "Seal up what the seven thunders have said and do not write it down." Then the angel I had seen standing on the sea and on the land raised his right hand to heaven. And he swore by him who lives for ever and ever, who created the heavens and all that is in them, the earth and all that is in it, and the sea and all that is in it, and said, "There will be no more delay! But in the days when the seventh angel is about to sound his trumpet, the mystery of God will be accomplished, just as he announced to His servants the prophets." Then the voice that I had heard from heaven spoke to me once more: "Go take the scroll that lies open in the hand of the angel who is standing on the sea and on the land." So I went to the angel and asked him to give me the little scroll. He said to me "take it and eat it. It will turn your stomach sour, but in your mouth it will be as sweet as honey." I took the little scroll from the angel's hand and ate it. It tasted as sweet as honey in my mouth, but when I had it, my stomach turned sour. Then I was told, "You must prophesy again about many peoples, nations, languages and kings." Revelation 10:1-11

The key verses for us in this passage are 6-7

'And the angel said, "There will be no more delay! But in the days when the seventh angel is about to sound his trumpet, the mystery of God will be accomplished, just as he announced to his servants the prophets." So what is the mystery of God, revealed to the prophets, that will unfold when the angel sounds the seventh trumpet?'

Daniel gives us the answer

'Seventy "sevens" are decreed for your people and your holy city to finish transgressions, to put an end to sin, to atone for wickedness, to bring in

everlasting righteousness, to seal up vision and prophecy and to anoint the most holy. Know and understand this: From the issuing of the decree to restore and rebuild Jerusalem until the Anointed One, the ruler, comes there will be seven "sevens," and sixty-two "sevens." It will be rebuilt with streets and a trench, but in times of trouble. After the sixty-two "sevens," the Anointed one will be cut off and will have nothing. The people of the ruler who will come will destroy the city and the sanctuary. The end will come like a flood: War will continue to the end, and desolations have been decreed. He will confirm a covenant with many for one "seven." In the middle of the "seven" he will put an end to sacrifice and offering. And on a wing of the temple he will set up an abomination that causes desolation, until the end that is decreed is poured out on him.' Daniel 9:24-27

The mystery God revealed to the prophets
The Anointed One will come twice: the first time after sixty-two "sevens," but will be cut off, and have nothing, as far as the Jews are concerned.

'He came to that which was his own, but his own did not receive him. Yet to all who received him, to those he gave the right to become children of God.' John 1:11

We need to grasp what the two comings of the Anointed One reveals to us
When He came the first time he came as a Jew: He came to his own, but his own did not receive him - He was crucified; a once for all sacrifice for sin (a Saviour) for those who believe in Him, but rejected as Messiah by the Jews. He returns the second time as Kinsman-Redeemer.

His second coming at the end of the sixty-nine "sevens" is for the Jews.

'Seventy "sevens" are decreed for your people (Daniel's people) and your holy city (Jerusalem) to finish transgressions, to put

*with many for one "seven." In the middle of the "seven" he will put an end
to sacrifice and offering. And on a wing of the temple he will set up an
abomination that causes desolation, until the end that is decreed is poured
out on him.'* Daniel 9:26-27

Paul gives us these words
*'Concerning the coming of our Lord Jesus Christ and our being gathered
to him, we ask you, brothers, not to become unsettled or alarmed by
some prophecy, report or letter supposed to have come from us, saying
that the day of the Lord has already come. Don't let anyone deceive you
in any way, for that day will not come until the rebellion occurs and the
man of lawlessness is revealed, the man doomed to destruction. He will
oppose and will exalt himself over everything that is called God or is
worshipped, so he sets himself up in God's temple, proclaiming himself to
be God.'* 2 Thessalonians 2:1-4

Who is it?
None other than the Antichrist; surely only he, his coming, would
be linked in this way to the coming of the Anointed One. Only the
Antichrist would set himself up in God's temple claiming to be God
and, Paul tells us, he comes when the rebellion occurs just before the
midpoint of the "seven."

The mystery God revealed to the prophets
The Lord would come twice, and he would come the second time
at the end of the last seven years of the Feast of Weeks, at the Feast
of Trumpets. The Antichrist would come when the rebellion against
God occurs. Also keep in mind the last seven years of the Feast of
Weeks, is not the seven-year covenant of the Antichrist, although they
are the same time-period.

After the seventh trumpet event, John is to prophesy again about
many peoples, nations, and kings. The beginning of the end; the
final seven-year period decreed for the children of Israel, in which the

mystery of God will be accomplished. But before the seventh trumpet sounds, we are given the second of the three woes.

The second woe begins and continues for 1,260 days - Gods two witnesses

'I was given a reed like a measuring rod and was told, "Go and measure the temple of God and the altar, and count the worshippers there. But exclude the outer court; do not measure it, because it has been given to the gentiles. They will trample on the holy city for forty-two months. And I will give power to my two witnesses, and they will prophesy for 1,260 days, clothed in sackcloth." These are the two olive trees and the two lamp stands that stand before the Lord of the earth. If anyone wants to harm them, fire comes out of their mouths and devours their enemies. This is how anyone who wants to harm them must die. These men have power to shut up the sky so that it will not rain during the time they are prophesying; and they have power to turn water into blood and to strike the earth with every kind of plague as often as they want.' Revelation 11:1-6

The beginning of the end

We are at the end of the beginning, and about to enter the beginning of the end. We are about to enter the sixty-ninth week of years of the seventy, decreed for the people of Israel, which is also the last week of years of the Feast of Weeks. This is a most suitable time, because of what is to come, for God to send two angels to bear witness for Him. There is the temptation to take the 1,260 days the two witnesses are to prophesy, to be half of the seven years, but the seven years will not begin until the seventh trumpet sounds. So why does this event come at this time, a few days before the fourth seal is opened? And why is the period of time given in a precise number of days rather than months, or times, two times, and half a time. The length of time the two witnesses prophesy is given in days, so that it starts and finishes at the right time in the order of events. If we speak of something happening in so many days, we state a definite date for that event to happen. But if we say the event will happen in times and two times and half a time, a day or two either way is not a problem.

The 1260 days begin a number of days before the start of the last seven years of the Feast of Weeks, therefore it will end before the mid-point. It *fits in* with the last week of years to achieve a particular result. God's two witnesses appear just before the start of the last week of years; arrive in Jerusalem before the mid-point of the seven years. The beast that comes up from the Abyss overpowers and kills them; their death is just after the armies of the beast desecrates the temple, and sets up the abomination which causes desolation; encouraging men everywhere to rebel against the God of Heaven.

Why must their death take place before the mid-point of the seven years? The second woe has begun and will continue for 1260 days.

CHAPTER 8

The Fourth Seal | The Seventh Trumpet

The seventh trumpet sounds - The mystery of God begins to be revealed

The last week of years of the Feast of Weeks, which is also the sixty-ninth week of years of the seventy "sevens" decreed for the Children of Israel begins. God's plan does not falter, and the outcome is certain: The beginning of the end is proclaimed with rejoicing in heaven.

The Heavenly Acclamation

'*The seventh angel sounded his trumpet, and there were loud voices in heaven, which said: "the kingdom of the world has become the kingdom of our Lord and of his Christ, and he will reign for ever." And the twenty-four elders, who were seated on their thrones before God, fell on their faces and worshipped God, saying: "we give thanks to you Lord God Almighty, the One who is and who was, because you have taken your great power and have begun to reign. The nations were angry; and your wrath has come. The time has come for judging the dead, and for rewarding your servants the prophets and your saints and those who reverence your name, both small and great - and for destroying those who destroy the earth." Then God's temple in heaven was opened, and within his temple was seen the ark of his covenant. And there came flashes of lightning, rumblings, peals of thunder, an earthquake and a great hailstorm.*' Revelation 11:15-19

The fourth seal is opened - the king named Death rides forth

'When the Lamb opened the fourth seal, I heard the voice of the fourth living creature say, "Come!" I looked and there before me was a pale horse! Its rider was named Death, and Hades was following close behind him. They were given power over a fourth of the earth to kill by sword, famine and plague, and by the wild beasts of the earth.' Revelation 6:7

The beast out of the sea

'And I saw a beast coming out of the sea. He had ten horns and seven heads, with ten crowns on his horns, and on each head a blasphemous name. The beast I saw resembled a leopard, but had feet like a bear and a mouth like that of a lion. The dragon gave the beast his power and his throne and great authority.' Revelation 13:1-2

The Kingdom

'After that, in my vision at night I looked, and there before me was a fourth beast - terrifying and frightening and very powerful. It had large iron teeth; it crushed and devoured its victims and trampled underfoot whatever was left. It was different from all the other beasts, and it had ten horns.' Daniel 7:7

Daniel asked an angel the true meaning of his visions and is given this explanation

'The fourth beast is a fourth kingdom that will appear on earth. It will be different from all the other kingdoms, and will devour the whole earth, trampling it down and crushing it. The ten horns are ten kings who will come from this kingdom. After them another king will arise different from the earlier ones; he will subdue three kings. He will speak against the Most High and oppress his saints and try to change the set times and the laws. The saints are handed over to him for a time, times and half a time.' Daniel 7:23-27

The king of the fourth beast - the horn that started small

'The goat became very great, but at the height of his power his large horn was broken off, and in its place four prominent horns grew up toward

the four winds of heaven. Out of one of them came another horn which started small but grew in power to the south and to the east and toward the beautiful land. It grew until it reached the host of heaven, and it threw some of the starry host down to the earth and trampled on them. It set itself up to be as great as the Prince of the Host; it took away the daily sacrifice from Him, and the place of his sanctuary was brought low. Because of rebellion, the host of the saints and the daily sacrifice were given over to it. It prospered in everything it did, and truth was thrown to the ground.' Daniel 8:8-12

The passage that says it all - a king and kingdom different from the rest

'He said (an angel) "I am going to tell you what will happen later in the time of wrath, because the vision concerns the appointed time of the end. The two horned ram that you saw represents the kings of Media and Persia. The shaggy goat is the king of Greece, and the large horn between his eyes is the first king. The four horns that replace the one that was broken off represents four kingdoms that will emerge from his nation but will not have the same power. In the latter part of their reign, when rebels have become completely wicked, a stern-faced king, a master of intrigue, will arise. He will become very strong, but not by his own power. He will cause astounding devastation and will succeed in whatever he does. He will destroy the mighty men and the holy people. He will cause deceit to prosper, and he will consider himself superior. When they feel secure, he will destroy many and take his stand against the Prince of princes. Yet he will be destroyed, but not by human power.' Daniel 8:19-25

So where does his power come from

'... The dragon gave the beast his power and his throne and great authority. The beast was given a mouth to utter proud words and blasphemies, and to exercise his authority for forty-two months. He opened his mouth to blaspheme God, and to slander his name and his dwelling place and those who live in heaven. He was given power to make war against the saints and to conquer them. And he was given authority over every tribe, people, language and nation. All inhabitants of the earth will worship

the beast - all whose names have not been written in the book of life belonging to the Lamb that was slain from the creation of the world.' Revelation 13:2b, 5-8

At this moment, to the beast out of the sea, satan gave his power, his throne, and great authority for forty-two months; yet he remains until the end of the seven years. At this time, he will take his stand against the Prince of princes, and be destroyed; but not by human hands.

The rider named Death: the king of the North, with Hades following close behind

'Then I saw a second beast coming out of the earth. He had two horns like a lamb, but spoke like a dragon. He exercised all the authority of the first beast on his behalf, and made the earth and its inhabitants worship the first beast, whose fatal wound had been healed. And he performed great and miraculous signs, even causing fire to come down from heaven to earth in full view of men. Because of the signs he was given to do on behalf of the first beast, he deceived the inhabitants of the earth...' Revelation 13:11-14

The two beasts work together, the beast out of the sea in power with the beast out of the earth - the false prophet – exercising all authority on behalf of the first beast. Someone who looks like a lamb, and deceives the inhabitants of the earth into satanic worship; preparing the way for satan's coming rule on earth to begin.

'The coming of the lawless one will be in accordance with the work of satan displayed with all kinds of counterfeit miracles, signs and wonders, and in every sort of evil that deceives those who are perishing. They perish because they refuse to love the truth and be saved.' 2 Thessalonian 2:9-10

We have opened four seals and revealed Daniel's four kingdoms, and the king named death, who has satanic powers: the contemptible person of Daniel's chronicle of the kings, who is given power over a fourth of the earth to kill by sword and famine.

The Fourth Seal: A pale horse, with a rider named Death, with Hades following close behind.

The Seventh Trumpet: A beast out of the sea, with a beast out of the earth.

The Chronicle of the Kings: A contemptible person.

We have reached the last week of years of the Feast of Weeks. What is written on the second side of the scroll begins.

CHAPTER 9

The Fifth Seal | The Firstfruits
The Three Angels

In the previous chapter we were reminded of Israel's favour with God, and as our focus is on the order of events, I asked the question. "Why does this affirmation of Israel come in the order of events at this time?" The answer is in what is about to come.

John sees the Lamb and with him the 144,000 men from the twelve tribes of Israel

'Then I looked, and there before me was the Lamb, standing on Mount Zion, and with him 144,000 who had his name and his Father's name written on their foreheads. And I heard a sound from heaven like the roar of rushing waters and like a loud peal of thunder. The sound I heard was like that of harpists playing their harps. And they sang a new song before the throne and before the four living creatures and the elders. No one could learn the song except the 144,000 who had been redeemed from the earth. These are those who did not defile themselves with women, for they kept themselves pure. They follow the lamb wherever he goes. They were purchased from among men and offered as firstfruits to God and the Lamb. No lie was found in their mouths; they are blameless.' Revelation 14:1-5

I have heard some debate about whether there is a secret rapture, or not, when or before the Lord returns; this event gives us the answer.

The Israelites celebrate the Feast of weeks with the firstfruits of the wheat harvest and the Feast of Ingathering at the turn of the year. (Exodus 34:22) The Feast of Weeks is a period of forty- nine years that begin when the first seal of the revelation is opened. This event takes place on the fiftieth day of the forty- third year – the first year of the last seven years before the Lord returns at the end of the Feast of weeks.

'Count of seven sabbaths of years – seven times seven years – so that the seven sabbaths of years amount to a period of forty-nine years. - From the day after the sabbath, the day you brought the wave offering, count of seven full weeks. Count off fifty days up to the day after the seventh sabbath, and then present an offering of new grain to the Lord.' Leviticus 25:8; 20:15

The shadow is past; what was foretold has come. God accepts 144,000 men (new grain) redeemed from the twelve tribes of Israel; from the same crop as the wave sheaf, the first of the firstfruits. (the Seven Feasts of Jehovah.)

Paul writes
'For since death came through a man, the resurrection of the dead comes also through a man. For as in Adam all die, so in Christ shall all be made alive. But each in his own turn: Christ; the firstfruits; then, when he comes those who belong to him. Then the end will come, when he hands over the kingdom to God the Father after he has destroyed all dominion, authority and power.' 1 Corinthians 15:21-25

This, then, is the order: first Christ; next, the firstfruits; then, when He comes, those who belong to Him. So we can say: Yes, there is a secret rapture before the Lord returns with the armies of heaven, for as the Lord took Enoch who walked with God (Genesis 5:24), 144,000 men of Israel will be taken, as firstfruits of the harvest that is to come. It will be secret as far as the Lord's appearance on mount Zion with the 144,000, unseen by the world, but revealed to John so that it could be written down and known by those who know their God and His word. These are the firstfruits of the harvest the Lord reaps from His chosen people, followed by the Feast of Ingathering at the turn of the year; the harvest of the earth.

After the firstfruits are accepted by God, He sends forth three angels, each with a different message.

The first angel

'Then I saw another angel flying in mid-air, and he had the eternal gospel to proclaim to those who live on earth - to every nation, tribe, language and people. He said in a loud voice, "fear God and give him the glory, because the hour of his judgement has come. Worship him who made the heavens, the earth, the sea and the springs of water." Revelation 14:6-18

At this point in the revelation, we have entered the last chance time for people everywhere to repent. The firstfruits are gathered; the harvest of the earth is at hand; God fulfils the great commission.

'And this gospel of the kingdom will be preached in the whole world as a testimony to all nations, and then the end will come.' Matthew 24:14

What the church on earth endeavoured to do, God now sends an angel to do for Him, so that men everywhere are without excuse.

'A second angel followed and said, "Fallen! Fallen is Babylon the Great, which made all the nations drink the maddening wine of her adulteries." Revelation 14:8

So much detail is given to us about Babylon the Great in the book of Revelation that we need to be aware of what Scripture has to say about her. And there has been much speculation about who she represents. Who is she? Why does her destruction bring shouts of Hallelujah! in heaven? Why is she singled out in this way by God for destruction?

Why is her destruction the last act of God's wrath, before the coming of the King of kings and the Lord of Lords? By the grace of God, we will find answers to these questions in a separate study. But here we see the certainty of her destruction foretold in this proclamation that focuses our attention on her making all the nations drink the maddening wine of her adulteries.

'A third angel followed them and said in a loud voice: "If anyone worships the beast and his image and receives his mark on the forehead or on the hand, he, too will drink of the wine of God's fury, which has been poured full strength into the cup of his wrath. He will be tormented with burning sulphur in the presence of the holy angels and of the Lamb. And the smoke of their torment rises for ever and ever. There is no rest day or night for those who worship the beast and his image, or for anyone who receives the mark of his name." This calls for patient endurance on the part of the saints who obey God's commandments and remain faithful to Jesus.' Revelation 14:9-12

As the angel finishes his warning not to worship satan, the fifth seal is opened

'When he opened the fifth seal, I saw under the altar the souls of those who had been slain because of the word of God and the testimony they had maintained. They called out in a loud voice, "How long Sovereign Lord, holy and true, until you judge the inhabitants of the earth and avenge our blood?" Then each of them was given a white robe, and they were told to wait a little longer, until the number of their fellow servants and brothers who were to be killed as they had been was completed.' Revelation 6:9-11

Then John hears a voice responding from heaven

Then I heard a voice from heaven say, "Blessed are the dead who die in the Lord from now on." "Yes" says the Spirit, "they will rest from their labour, for their deeds will follow them." Revelation 14:13

When the beast, the king with satanic power, comes to rule (when the seventh trumpet sounds at the beginning of the last week of years) he makes war against the saints and kills many of them during his 42 months in power. The souls under the altar are those killed by him up to the fifth seal event, when they are told to wait a little longer until their number is made complete, when the Prince of this world comes at the Harvest of the Earth.

The fifth seal is unique in that it is the only one that occurs in heaven and the response to it is from heaven. This seal event and the response confirm, by their positions in different columns in the table of events, that the sequence of events so far is correct.

CHAPTER 10

The Rebellion Against God
The Rule of satan Begins

We are at the point in Daniel's chronicle of the kings where the rebellion against God takes place. The firstfruits are gathered; the gospel has been preached to the whole world; the warnings given; the crop is ripe for harvest; the man of lawlessness is about to be revealed. Blessed are the dead who die in the Lord from now on.

The beast out of the sea receives authority for forty-two months
'The beast was given a mouth to utter proud words and blasphemies and to exercise his authority for forty two months. He opened his mouth to blaspheme God, and to slander his name and his dwelling place, and those who live in heaven. He was given power to make war against the saints and to conquer them. And he was given authority over every tribe, people, language, and nation. All the inhabitants of the earth will worship the beast - all whose names have not been written in the book of life belonging to the Lamb that was slain from the creation of the world.'
Revelation 13:5-8

The beast out of the sea, the king of the North, who came to power at the beginning of the last week of years, now comes to the end of his forty two months of authority; in one sense at an end, but he remains to serve his master.

Who will rule the northern kingdom? - Paul gives us the answer.

The coming of the man of lawlessness

'Concerning the coming of our Lord Jesus Christ and our being gathered to Him, we ask you brothers not to become easily unsettled or alarmed by some prophecy, report or letter supposed to have come from us, saying that the day of the Lord has already come. Don't let anyone deceive you in any way. For that day will not come until the rebellion occurs and the man of lawlessness is revealed, the man doomed to destruction. He will oppose and will exalt himself over everything that is called God or is worshipped, so that he sets himself up in God's temple, proclaiming himself to be God. Don't you remember that when I was with you I used to tell you these things? And now you know what is holding him back, so that he may be revealed at the proper time. For the secret power of lawlessness is already at work; but the one who now holds it back will continue to do so till he is taken out of the way. And then the lawless one will be revealed, whom the Lord Jesus will overthrow with the breath of his mouth and destroy with the splendour of his coming.' 2 Thessalonians 2:1-8

Paul writes: "The day will not come until the rebellion occurs and the man of lawlessness is revealed." Another person is revealed when the one who holds him back is taken out of the way. We have reached the point in Daniel's chronicle of the kings, where the armies of the king of the north rise up and desecrate the temple fortress; abolish the daily sacrifice, and set up the abomination that causes desolation, and the rebellion occurs. This is almost the mid-point of the seven years; the king of the north sets up an image of himself as the Prince of Hosts; his authority comes to an end, for the time has come for the man of lawlessness to be revealed. The Holy Spirit leaves the world to satan and the powers of darkness.

It is the coming of satan which holds the interest of the angels

'Then I heard a holy one speaking, and another holy one said to him, "How long will it take for the vision to be fulfilled - the vision concerning the daily sacrifice, the rebellion that causes desolation, and the surrender of the sanctuary and of the host that will be trampled underfoot?" He said

to me, *"It will take 2,300 evenings and mornings: then the sanctuary will be re-consecrated."* Daniel 8:13-14

The sanctuary is surrendered to the man of lawlessness, the beast who came up from the Abyss, whose absolute rule on earth begins for the second half of the last seven years decreed for the children of Israel. However, the beast out of the sea and the beast out of the earth remain to make the trinity on earth complete.

Then John looked and saw the Harvest of the Earth - The Feast of Ingathering

'I looked and there before me was a white cloud, and seated on the cloud was one "like the son of man" with a crown of gold on his head and a sharp sickle in his hand. Then another angel came out of the temple and called in a loud voice to him who was seated on the cloud, "Take your sickle and reap, because the time to reap has come, for the harvest of the earth is ripe." So he who was seated on the cloud swung his sickle over the earth, and the earth was harvested.' Revelation 14:14-16

The harvest of grapes for the winepress of God's wrath

'Another angel came out of the temple in heaven, and he too had a sharp sickle. Still another angel, who had charge of the fire, came from the altar and called in a loud voice to him who had the sharp sickle, "Take your sharp sickle and gather the clusters of grapes from the earth's vine, because its grapes are ripe." The angel swung his sickle on the earth, gathered its grapes and threw them into the great wine press of God's wrath. They were trampled in the wine press outside the city, and the blood flowed out of the press, rising as high as the horses' bridles for a distance of 1,6000 Stadia.' Revelation 14:17-20

With a first reading of this vision, it would seem that it could be a symbolic way of expressing the coming of the Lord. However, this is the fulfilment of the Feast of Ingathering. (See supplementary study, "The Feasts of Jehovah".) There are two harvesters, with a crop to harvest, and a crop to be gathered; both expressed in a symbolic way. That does not mean they are only symbolic: for they must take place as events, in the order of events; but not by angels swinging sharp sickles. The first harvester, and he must harvest first, is "one like the son of man" with a crown of gold on his head; he took his sickle and harvested the earth. It is he who harvests the earth before the coming wrath of God. So who is the harvester? What is the crop? Remember we are almost at the mid-point of the final seven years; things are moving at a fast pace; the end will come like a flood. The fifth seal is opened; the souls under the altar are told to wait a little longer until the number of their fellow servants and brothers to be killed was complete. The Holy Spirit has been taken out of the way to allow the prince of this world to come, and all who know and love the Lord at this time are put to death: The earth is harvested; the elect gathered to be with the souls under the altar to make their number complete.

Now hold on a minute!
The Lord must appear before the elect are gathered to meet with Him in the air. This is no resurrection, but the harvest of the earth; not heaven and earth. Keep in mind that there are two harvesters, neither of which is the Lord. However, one of them is like the Son of Man, with a golden crown on his head: the (angel of the) Holy Spirit. The Holy Spirit, the harvester, taken out of the way, allows the harvest to take place. The man of lawlessness comes. He sets himself up in God's temple, proclaims himself to be God, slays God's holy people. Can there be any Christians left on earth in satan's kingdom? I think not. Would God ask the elect to pay the price of sin on their own behalf; suffer His wrath? That price has already been paid, thanks be to God for the Lord Jesus Christ.

Jesus said." If those days had not been cut short, no one would survive, but for the sake of the elect, those days will be shortened." Matthew 24:22

The second woe comes to its end: the death of God's two witnesses
'I will give power to my two witnesses, and they will prophesy for 1260

days, clothed in sackcloth. These are the two olive trees and the two lampstands that stand before the Lord of the earth. Now when they have finished their testimony, the beast that comes up from the Abyss will attack them and overpower and kill them. Their bodies will lie in street of the great city, which is figuratively called Sodom and Egypt, where also their Lord was crucified. For three and a half days men from every people, tribe language and nation will gaze on their bodies and refuse them burial.'
Revelation 11:3-4

'The inhabitants of the earth will gloat over them and will celebrate by sending each other gifts, because these two prophets had tormented those who live on the earth. But after three and a half days a breath of life from God entered them, and they stood on their feet, and terror struck those who saw them. Then they heard a loud voice from heaven saying to them, "Come up here." And they went up to heaven in a cloud while their enemies looked on. At that very hour there was a severe earthquake, and a tenth of the city collapsed. Seven thousand people were killed in the earthquake, and the survivors were terrified and gave glory to the God of heaven.' Revelation 11:7-14

The power of the holy people is finally broken; all is complete
'Then I, Daniel, looked, and there before me stood two others, one on this bank of the river and one on the opposite bank. One of them said to the man clothed in linen, who was above the waters of the river, "How long will it be before these astonishing things are fulfilled?" The man clothed in linen, who was above the waters of the river, lifted his left hand toward heaven, and I heard him swear by him who lives forever, saying, "It will be for a time, times and half a time. When the power of the holy people has been finally broken, all these things will be completed." Daniel 12:5-7

The Holy Spirit has been taken out of the world, and His harvest, the death of all Christians, takes place; those who remain after the 42 months reign of the satanic king. Now satan has come to power, and kills them and God's two witnesses: he would not, could not, in accordance with his nature, linger, but act. No one but satan could kill them, because they were angels, not even the false prophet who can perform signs and wonders, or the beast out of the sea, the king who magnifies himself over every god. Now we can understand why they came to earth just before the last seven years begin. They had to be in Jerusalem, their testimony finished, as satan came to rule over a rebellious world. Their death, the last event, to complete all things, before God's wrath begins.

When the Holy Spirit is taken out of the way; the prince of this world comes just as Jesus said he would. We may find it difficult to accept that the world is given over to satan who Paul says sets himself up in God's temple as God; his visible presence on earth. And there appears to be some difficulty between the translations of the N.I.V. and the R.S.V. which centres around who causes the desolations that follow the coming of the man of lawlessness. And did another person come when the rebellion occurs?

In the New International Version, it states - he will set up an abomination that causes desolation.
'...*the people of the ruler who will come will destroy the city and the sanctuary. The end will come like a flood: War will continue to the end, and desolations have been decreed. He will confirm a covenant with many for one "seven". In the middle of the "seven" he will put an end to sacrifice and offering. And on a wing of the temple he will set up an abomination that causes desolation, until the end that is decreed is poured out on him.'*
Daniel 9:26-27

The N.I.V. says the people of the ruler who will come will set up an abomination that causes desolation. This suggests that this ruler is the beast out of the sea, the king of the north, who made the covenant, and set up the image in the temple. However, "the *people* of the ruler who will come" could include the beast out of the sea whose authority ends after 42 months. This would account for the change of authority that must take place at this time, but leaves unresolved who caused the desolations, the person who came, or the image set up in the temple.

In the R.S.V. we have another person coming - a Prince who will cause desolation

'The people of the prince who is to come shall destroy the city and the sanctuary. Its end shall come with a flood, and to the end there shall be war; desolations are decreed. And he shall make a strong covenant with many for one week; and for half the week he shall cause sacrifice and offering to cease; and upon the wing of abominations shall come "one" who makes desolate, until the decreed end is poured out on the desolater.'
Daniel 9:26-27

In the R.S.V. we have: The people of the prince who is to come - upon the wing of abominations shall come *one* who makes desolate. This brings another person unto the scene, one who is a prince, one who now takes authority and causes desolations. And can I say - "Upon the wing the fallen angelic desolater comes. This agrees with Paul, in that another person, the man of lawlessness, a prince, comes to set himself up in God's temple, proclaiming himself to be God. If we take this prince to be the beast out of the sea, the title of prince is not in keeping with what we know about him. He was not given the honour of royalty, and is called a contemptible person. (Daniel 11:21) The R.S.V. translation of these verses is easily understood. However, the N.I.V. translation that I used for the study needs to be understood in the context of the trinity It is a fact: satan gave his power, his throne, and great authority, to the beast out of the sea. He has come to power in the beast, but is still restrained until the rebellion occurs, and the one who restrains him (the Holy Spirit) is taken out of the way. Then satan comes to absolute power over the earth and everything in it. And with the beast out of the sea and the beast out of the earth they act like a trinity; they are one the beast is one. What is written in this context – the trinity – can begin with one person of the trinity and finish with another.

And I believe we can say

Daniel 12:11

'From the time the daily sacrifice is abolished and the abomination that causes desolation is set up, there will be 1,290 days. Blessed is the one who waits for and reaches the end of the 1,335 days.'

God's enemy, satan, comes to rule 1290 days before the end of the seven years - that is 1230 days from the beginning - 30 days before the mid-point. (mid-point - 42 months × 30 days=1260) And I believe - 'blessed is the one who waits for and reaches the end of the 1335 days' - is reference to the remnant of Israel - The Jews redeemed at the Lord's return - those who celebrate the Feast of Tabernacles at the beginning of His 1,000 year reign.

After the harvest of the earth, John is shown another heavenly sign

Revelation 15:1

'I saw in heaven another great and marvellous sign: seven angels with the seven last plagues – last, because with them God's wrath is completed.'

CHAPTER 11
The Sixth Seal
The Seven Bowls of God's Wrath

The Holy Spirit is taken out of the way.

The time when satan's rule on earth begins.

The earth is harvested; those who bore testimony to Jesus and the word of God put to death.

God's two witnesses killed.

The grapes of the earth gathered for the winepress of God's wrath.

The Lord's affirmation that all is safely gathered in before His wrath begins

'I saw in heaven another great and marvellous sign: seven angels with seven last plagues - last, because with them God's wrath is completed. And I saw what looked like a sea of glass mixed with fire, and standing beside the sea, those who had been victorious over the beast and his image and over the number of his name. They held harps given them by God and sang the song of Moses the servant of God and the song of the Lamb. "Great and marvellous are your deeds, Lord God Almighty. Just and true are your ways, King of the ages. Who will not fear you, O Lord, and bring glory to your name? For you alone are holy. All nations will come and worship before you, for your righteous acts have been revealed." Revelation 15:1-4

John is shown the vision of the wrath to come

'After this I looked and in heaven the temple, that is, the tabernacle of

the Testimony, was opened. Out of the temple came the seven angels with the seven last plagues. They were dressed in clean, shining linen and wore golden sashes around their chests. Then one of the four living creatures gave to the seven angels seven golden bowls filled with the wrath of God, who lives for ever and ever. And the temple was filled with smoke from the glory of God and from his power, and no one could enter the temple until the seven plagues of the seven angels were completed.' Revelation 15:5-8

'Then I heard a voice from the temple saying to the seven angels, "Go pour out the seven bowls of God's wrath on the earth." Revelation 16:1

The first angel *went and poured out his bowl on the land, and ugly and painful sores broke out on the people who had the mark of the beast and worshipped his image.* Revelation 16:2

The second angel *poured out his bowl on the sea, and it turned into blood like that of a dead man, and every living thing in the sea died.* Revelation 16:3

The third angel *poured out his bowl on the rivers and springs of water, and they became blood. Then I heard the angel in charge of the waters say: "You are just in these judgements, you who are and who were, the Holy One, because you have so judged; for they have shed the blood of your saints and prophets, and you have given them blood to drink as they deserve." And I heard the altar respond: "Yes Lord God Almighty, true and just are your judgements."* Revelation 16:4-7

The fourth angel *poured out his bowl on the sun, and the sun was given power to scorch people with fire. They were seared by the intense heat and they cursed the name of God, who had control of these plagues, but they refused to repent and glorify him.* Revelation 16:8-9

The fifth angel *poured out his bowl on the throne of the beast, and his kingdom was plunged into darkness. Men gnawed their tongues in agony* *and cursed the God of heaven because of their pains and their sores, but they refused to repent of what they had done.* Revelation 16:10-11

God's wrath comes with unstoppable relentless purpose, and begins with ugly painful sores on those who bore the mark of the beast. This is of some interest because the time of woe began when satan was permitted to harm, with painful sores, those who did not have the seal of God on their foreheads. And we could speculate about the sea, the springs of waters, and the rivers (whether they were actually turned to blood), and whether those left on earth were given blood to drink because they shed the blood of prophets and saints (blood symbolising God's judgement). But whatever, everything in the sea is dead, the sun has power to scorch and sear men, and the northern kingdom has been plunged into darkness. Perhaps we should ask: what would be the consequences for the world and its inhabitants? However: we need not speculate.

'See the Lord is going to lay waste the earth and devastate it; He will ruin its face and scatter its inhabitants. The earth will be completely laid waste and totally plundered. The earth dries up and withers, the world languishes and withers, the exalted of the earth languish. The earth is defiled by its people; they have disobeyed the laws, violated the statues and broken the everlasting covenant. Therefore a curse consumes the earth; its people must bear their guilt. Therefore earth's inhabitants are burned up and very few are left.' Isaiah 24:1; 24:3-6

God's judgement on a sinful world is true and just for they cursed him because of their suffering and refused to repent of what they had done. A world that turned its back in rebellion against its Creator God defiled the earth, broke the everlasting covenant, and worshipped satan. God's timing and where the events take place are perfect, but some of them, like the trumpet events, cannot be placed precisely in our table of events. However, the sixth bowl of wrath enables us to place the others in relative positions.

The sixth bowl of God's wrath

'The sixth angel poured out his bowl on the great river Euphrates, and its water was dried up to prepare the way for the kings from the east. Then I saw three evil spirits that looked like frogs; they came out of the mouth of the dragon, out of the mouth of the beast and out of mouth of the false prophet. They are spirits of demons performing miraculous signs, and they go out to the kings of the whole world, to gather them for the battle on the great day of God Almighty "Behold I come like a thief! Blessed is he who stays awake and keeps his clothes with him, so that he may not go naked and be shamefully exposed." Then they gathered the kings together to the place that in Hebrew is called Armageddon.' Revelation 16:12-16

We can place this event opposite that part in the column of kings, where the last war between the North and the South takes place. The king of the North wins and makes camp between the seas at the Holy Mountain, and from there the kings of the earth will be gathered at Armageddon. We have reached the point in Daniel's chronicle of the kings, when the final battle between the north and south is at an end.

'At the time of the end the king of the South will engage him in battle, and the king of the North will storm out against him with chariots and cavalry and a great fleet of ships. He will invade many countries and sweep through them like a flood. He will also invade the Beautiful Land. Many countries will fall, but Edom, Moab and the leaders of Ammon will be delivered from his hand. He will extend his power over many countries; Egypt will not escape. He will gain control of the treasures of gold and silver and all the riches of Egypt, with the Libyans and Nubians in submission. But reports from the east and the north will alarm him, and he will set out in a great rage to destroy and annihilate many. He will pitch his tents between the seas at the beautiful holy mountain. Yet he will come to his end, and no one will help him.' Daniel 11:40-44

Now the scene is almost set for the coming of the King of Kings, but the rest of mankind needs to be drawn into the preparations for

Armageddon. So satan sends out three evil spirits of demons, one from himself, one from the beast out of the sea, and one from the beast out of the earth. Performing miraculous signs, they go out to the whole world, to gather them for battle on the great day of God Almighty. But before the King of Kings comes, the sixth seal opens, and the seventh bowl of God's wrath pours out.

There are two major parallel events
The first is the fourth seal: the seventh trumpet
The second is the sixth seal: the seventh bowl of God's wrath

The sixth Seal
'I watched as he opened the sixth seal. There was a great earthquake. The sun turned black like sackcloth made of goat hair, the whole moon turned blood red, and the stars in the sky fell to earth, as late figs drop from a fig tree when shaken by a strong wind. The sky receded like a scroll, rolling up, and every mountain and island was removed from its place. The kings of the earth, the princes, the generals, the rich, the mighty, and every slave and every free man hid in caves and among the rocks of the mountains. They called to the mountains and the rocks, "Fall on us and hide us from the face of him who sits on the throne and from the wrath of the Lamb! For the great day of their wrath has come, and who can stand?" Revelation 6:12-17

Like the previous seal event, there is no mystery about this one, an earthquake that affects the whole world, and may be the result of cosmic activity, or has itself made the earth reel like a drunkard; its movement through space causing the sky to appear to recede like a scroll rolling up. This event finds its "parallel" in the seventh bowl of God's wrath.

The seventh bowl of God's wrath
'The seventh angel poured out his bowl into the air, and out of the temple came a loud voice from the throne, saying, "It is done!" Then there came

flashes of lightning, rumblings, peals of thunder and a severe earthquake. No earthquake like it has ever occurred since man has been on earth, so tremendous was the quake. The great city split into three parts, and the cities of the nations collapsed. God remembered Babylon the Great and gave her the cup filled with the wine of the fury of his wrath. Every island fled away and the mountains could not be found. From the sky huge hailstones of about a hundred pounds each fell upon men. And they cursed God on account of the plague of hail, because the plague was so terrible.' Revelation 16:17-21

We cannot ignore what the prophet Isaiah writes about this earthquake; for in that day the Lord will reign

'The floodgates of heaven are opened, the foundations of the earth shake. The earth is broken up, the earth is split asunder, the earth is thoroughly shaken. The earth reels like a drunkard, it sways like a hut in the wind; so heavy upon it is the guilt of its rebellion that it falls - never to rise again. In that day the Lord will punish the powers in heavens above and the earth below. They will be herded together like prisoners bound in a dungeon; they will be shut up in prison and be punished after many days. The moon will be abashed, the sun ashamed; for the Lord Almighty will reign on mount Zion and in Jerusalem, and before its elders gloriously.' Isaiah 24:18-23

This earthquake event heralds the Lord's second coming: 'In that day the Lord will punish the powers in the heavens above and the earth below, and the Lord Almighty will reign on mount Zion and in Jerusalem.' But God remembered one last thing: Babylon the Great, and the punishment due to her, for with it God's wrath ends.

The destruction of Babylon the Great

'The ten horns you saw are ten kings who have not yet received a kingdom, but for one hour will receive authority as kings along with the beast. They will make war against the Lamb, but the Lamb will overcome them because he is Lord of lords and King of kings - and with him will

be his called, chosen and faithful followers. Then the angel said to me, "The waters you saw, where the prostitute sits, are peoples, multitudes, nations and languages. The beast and the ten horns you saw will hate the prostitute. They will bring her to ruin and leave her naked; they will eat her flesh and burn her with fire. For God has put it into their hearts to accomplish his purpose by agreeing to give the beast their power to rule, until God's words are fulfilled. The woman you saw is the great city that rules over the kings of the earth." Revelation 17:12-18

When we begin to study the book of Revelation, it appears the wars are between the Middle East and Europe, and we are left wondering about all the other populated areas of the world that still remain. Well! Here we have what is left of them: ten kings representing the whole world, deceived by demons into giving their allegiance to the satanic forces; all in rebellion against the God of heaven. The whole rebellious world is gathered at Armageddon, ready to fight against the King of kings and the Lord of lords. Moreover they are united to bring destruction to Babylon the Great, for mighty is the Lord God who judges her. However, it was the beast with the ten horns who brought her to ruin. Why did God not destroy her himself? God has given the beast absolute power to rule on earth, for the present, until His word is fulfilled; so it is given to satan to destroy her. We know the beast and the ten kings hated the Mother of Prostitutes, but we do not know why. Perhaps she wanted her place at the table along with the ten kings. Whatever the reason, God's final act of wrath against a rebellious world is complete with the destruction of Babylon the Great, the Mother of Prostitutes, and of the Abominations of the Earth; making way for the opening of the seventh seal.

Before the seventh seal is opened, the heavens respond to Babylon's destruction

'After this I saw another angel coming down from heaven. He had great authority, and the earth was illuminated by his splendour. With

a mighty voice he shouted: Fallen! Fallen! is Babylon the great! She has become a home for demons and a haunt for every evil spirit, a haunt for every unclean and detestable bird. For all the nations have drunk the maddening wine of her adulteries. The kings of the earth committed adultery with her, and the merchants of the earth grew rich from her excessive luxuries." Then I heard another voice from heaven say: "Come out of her my people, so that you will not share in her sins, so that you will not receive any of her plagues; for her sins are piled up to heaven, and God has remembered her crimes. Give back to her as she has given; pay her back double for what she has done. Mix her a double portion from her own cup. Give her as much torture and grief as the glory and the luxury she gave herself. In her heart she boasts, "I sit as queen; I am not a widow, and I will never mourn." Therefore in one day her plagues will overtake her: death mourning and famine. She will be consumed by fire for mighty is the Lord who judges her.' Revelation 18:1-8

"Rejoice over her, O heaven!
'The roar of a great multitude in heaven shouting: Hallelujah! Salvation and glory and power belong to our God, for true and just are his judgements. He has condemned the great prostitute who corrupted the earth by her adulteries. He has avenged on her the blood of his servants." And again they shouted: "Hallelujah! The smoke from her goes up for ever and ever." The twenty four- elders and the four living creatures fell down and worshipped God, who was seated on the throne. And they cried "Amen, Hallelujah!" Revelation19:1- 4

So the Amen is given to the destruction of Babylon the Great; the end of God's wrath against a fallen world. An end to all the events that must take place before the seventh seal is opened, and the bridegroom comes.

The wedding of the Lamb proclaimed
'Then a voice came from the throne, saying: Praise our God, all you his servants, you who fear him, both small and great!" Then I heard what

sounded like a great multitude, like the roar of rushing waters and like loud peals of thunder, shouting: "Hallelujah! For our Lord God reigns. Let us rejoice and be glad and give him the glory! For the wedding of the lamb has come, and his bride has made herself ready. Fine linen, bright and clean, was given her to wear." (Fine linen stands for the righteous acts of the saints.) Then the angel said to me, "Write: Blessed are those who are invited to the wedding supper of the Lamb!" and he added, "These are the true words of God." At this I fell at his feet to worship him. But he said to me, "Do not do it! I am a fellow servant with you and with your brothers who hold to the testimony of Jesus. Worship God! For the testimony of Jesus is the spirit of prophecy." Revelation 19:5-10

All heaven praises God, for our Lord God reigns

The Feast of Weeks has ended; the Feast of Trumpets has come. The bride is made ready: the invitations are given; the bridegroom is coming.

CHAPTER 12

The Seventh Seal | The King of Kings

God's wrath on a rebellious world ends
The firstfruits of Israel are accepted by God; the harvest of the earth has gathered in the last of the Christians. God's wrath comes on a rebellious world ruled by satan, and ends with the punishment of Babylon the Great. The seventh seal is opened and Israel's Kinsman-Redeemer, Messiah, comes to reign.

The inhabitants of the earth know the end has come
'Then the kings of the earth, the princes, the generals, the rich, the mighty, and every slave and freeman hid in the caves and among the rocks, "Fall on us and hide us from the face of him who sits on the throne and from the wrath of the Lamb! For the great day of their wrath has come, and who can stand?" Revelation 6:15-17

The seventh seal opens with the immediacy of His coming
'When he opened the seventh seal, there was silence in heaven for half an hour. And I saw the seven angels who stand before God, and to them were given seven trumpets.' Revelation 8:1-2

Why does the opening of the seventh seal not record an event of its own, but shows John the seven angels with seven trumpets, that in turn call forth events when the first four seals are opened. Why is heaven silent for half an hour?

As the events take place, a stone is thrown; an event has occurred. There has to be a seventh seal event.

Would Jesus need to show John what was obvious? Would He announce his own coming? Or would he just come? Surely it would be the latter. And it is no coincidence, that when the seventh seal is shown to John it looks forward to the seven trumpets, for the Feast of Weeks ends when God's wrath is over, and the Feast of Trumpets heralds the coming of the King of Kings and the Lord of Lords who will reign on mount Zion and in Jerusalem.

'In that day the Lord will punish the powers in the heavens above and the earth below. They will be herded together like prisoners bound in a dungeon; they will be shut up in prison and be punished after many days. The moon will be abashed, the sun ashamed; for the Lord God Almighty will reign on mount Zion and in Jerusalem, and before its elders, gloriously.' Isaiah 24:21-23

The King of kings is coming to reign. Will he come like the other kings riding on a horse? If so, where is the horse? Where is the rider? What task to perform? Well! Here is the horse, here is the Rider: no need to wonder who He is; no need to contemplate His task; no need to ask of His kingdom or authority. This is the moment of anticipation, of expectation. So astounding is the event, so powerful, so majestic, that even heaven is silenced for half an hour.

The event that silences Heaven for half an hour?

'I saw heaven standing open and before me was a white horse, whose rider is called Faithful and true. With justice he judges and makes war. His eyes are like blazing fire, and on His head are many crowns. He has a name written on Him that no one knows but he himself. He is dressed in a robe dipped in blood, and his name is the Word of God. The armies of heaven were following him, riding on white horses and dressed in fine linen, white and clean. Out of his mouth comes a sharp sword with which

to strike down the nations. "He will rule them with an iron sceptre." He treads the wine press of the fury of the wrath of God Almighty. On his robe and on his thigh he has this name written: KING OF KINGS AND LORD OF LORDS. And I saw an angel standing in the sun, who cried in a loud voice to all the birds flying in mid-air, "Come, gather together for the great supper of God, so that you may eat the flesh of kings, generals, and mighty men, of horses and their riders, and the flesh of all people, free and slave, small and great." Then I saw the beast and the kings of the earth and their armies gathered together to make war against the rider on the horse and his army. But the beast was captured, and with him the false prophet who had performed the miraculous signs on his behalf. With these signs he had deluded those who had received the mark of the beast and worshipped his image. The two of them were thrown alive into the fiery lake of burning sulphur. The rest of them were killed with the sword that came out of the mouth of the rider on the horse, and all the birds gorged themselves on their flesh.' Revelation 19:11-21

The event that all creation feared and longed for has come. The rider is called Faithful and True, with justice He judges and makes war. His sign has appeared in the heavens; the elect are gathered from the four winds of heaven; their souls raised from the first death. Clothed in fine white linen; they ride out with the armies of heaven. We are given no indication of how the battle is fought; the outcome always certain; the defeat of the powers of darkness; the capture and destruction of the beast and the false prophet. Now the war is over, the elect raised from the first death, wait for the second resurrection. But we must not lose sight of the purpose of the Lord's second coming.

'He will appear a second time, not to bear sin, but to bring salvation to those who are waiting for him.' Hebrews 9:28

The Israelites wait for their kinsman Redeemer. The second coming of the Lord is a type of parallel event. It is the same event, from two perspectives, that we need to note, because the paths of salvation and redemption, entwined up to now, separate.

The Lord - Messiah - rules the nations from Jerusalem

'I will gather all the nations to Jerusalem to fight against it; the city will be captured, the houses ransacked, and the women raped. Half of the city will go into exile, but the rest of the people will not be taken from the city. Then the Lord will go out and fight against those nations, as he fights in the day of battle. On that day his feet will stand on the Mount of Olives, east of Jerusalem, and the mount of Olives will be split in two from east to west, forming a great valley, with half of the mountain moving north and half moving south. You will flee by my mountain valley, for it will extend to Azel. You will flee as you fled from the earthquake in the days of Uzziah king of Judah. Then the Lord my God will come, and all the holy ones with him. On that day there will be no light, no cold or frost. It will be an unique day, without daytime or night-time - a day known to the Lord. When evening comes, there will be light. On that day living water will flow out from Jerusalem, half to the eastern sea and half to the western sea, in summer and winter. The Lord will be King over the whole earth. On that day there will be one Lord, and his name the only name.'
Zechariah 14:2-9

'On that day I will set out to destroy all the nations that attack Jerusalem. And I will pour out on the house of David and the inhabitants of Jerusalem the Spirit of grace and supplication. They will look on me the one they pierced, and they will mourn for him as one mourns for an only child, and grieve bitterly for him as one grieves for a first born son.'
Zechariah 12:9-10

The war is over and satan is bound for a thousand years

'And I saw an angel coming down out of heaven, having the key to the Abyss and holding in his hand a great chain. He seized the dragon, that ancient serpent, who is the devil, or satan, and bound him for a thousand years. He threw him into the Abyss, and locked and sealed it over him, to keep him from deceiving the nations any more until the thousand years are ended. After that he must be set free for a short time.'
Revelation 20:1-3

The Lord's earthly reign begins with the resurrection of those who had not worshipped the beast.

'I saw thrones on which were seated those who had been given authority to judge. And I saw the souls of those who had been beheaded because of their testimony for Jesus and because of the word of God. They had not worshipped the beast or his image and had not received his mark on their foreheads or their hands. They came to life and reigned with Christ a thousand years. (the rest of the dead did not come to life until the thousand years were ended.) This is the first resurrection. Blessed and holy are those who have part in the first resurrection. The second death has no power over them, but they will be priests of God and of Christ and will reign with him for a thousand years.' Revelation 20:4-6

Blessed and holy are these - priests of God and of Christ

We know who these blessed people are. They have come through the most terrible times of persecution for their faith; the most devastating times of the earth's history; yet they have held fast to their testimony for Jesus and the Word of God; refusing the mark of the beast even unto death; reaped and united with the souls of those who were slain by the satanic king. Having a special place in God's heart, he gives them a great reward; the first to be resurrected, made alive, body and soul, to reign with Christ a thousand years. It is these and these alone who take part in the first resurrection. John first of all saw their souls, which were raised from the first death as spiritual beings and given white robes. Then they came to life: raised, body and soul; then they were judged; then reigned with Christ for a thousand years. They, and only they, are eternal beings, to be priests of God and of Christ.

The continuing disobedience of the nations

'Then the survivors from all the nations that have attacked Jerusalem will go up year after year to worship the King, the Lord Almighty, and to celebrate the Feast of Tabernacles. If any of the peoples of the earth do not go up to Jerusalem to worship the King, the Lord Almighty, they will have no rain. If the Egyptian people do not go up and take part, they

will have no rain. The Lord will bring on them the plagues he inflicts on the nations that do not go up to celebrate the Feast of Tabernacles.' Zechariah 14:16-19

What about the rest of mankind alive at this time, those who are not Jews, are they lost souls? Surely the Lord would give them a way of salvation during the thousand years of His earthly reign?

*'This is what Isaiah son of Amoz saw concerning Judah and Jerusalem: In the last days the mountain of the Lord's temple will be established as chief among the mountains; it will be raised above the hills, and all the nations will stream to it. Many peoples will come and say, "Come let us go up to the mountain of the Lord, to the house of the God of Jacob. **He will teach us his ways, so that we may walk in his paths.**"* Isaiah 2:1-4

The law will go out from Zion, the word of the Lord from Jerusalem. He will judge between the nations and will settle disputes for many peoples. They will beat their swords into ploughshares and their spears into pruning hooks. Nation will not take up sword against nation, nor will they train for war any more.

If you become a Jew are you saved?
"He will teach us his ways, so that we may walk in his paths." Isaiah 2:3

The Lord speaks through the prophet
"Shout and be glad, O Daughter of Zion. For I am coming, and I will live among you," declares the Lord. "Many nations will be joined with the Lord in that day and will become my people. I will live among you and you will know how the Lord Almighty has sent me to you." Zechariah 2:10-11

The Lord rules the nations - Jerusalem restored
'The Lord will be king over the whole earth. On that day there will be one Lord, and his name the only name. The whole land, from Geba to

Rimmon, south of Jerusalem, will be like the Arabah. But Jerusalem will be raised up and remain in its place, from the Benjamin Gate to the site of the First Gate, to the Corner Gate, and from the tower of Hananael to the royal wine press. It will be inhabited; never again will it be destroyed. Jerusalem will be secure.' Zechariah 14:9-11

God's people Israel dwell securely
'But you, Bethlehem Ephrathah, though you are small among the clans of Judah, out of you will come for me one who will be ruler over Israel, whose origins are from of old, from ancient times.' Micah 5:2

'He will stand and shepherd his flock in the strength of the Lord, in the majesty of the name of the Lord his God. And they will live securely, for then his greatness will reach to the ends of the earth. And he will be their peace.' Micah 5:4-5

The thousand years of Christ's rule on earth ends
When the thousand years are over, satan will be released from his prison, and will go out to deceive the nations in the four corners of the earth - Gog and Magog - to gather them for battle. In number they are like the sand on the seashore. They marched across the breadth of the earth and surrounded the camp of God's people, the city he loves. But fire came down from heaven and devoured them. And the devil, who deceived them, was thrown into the lake of burning sulphur where the beast and the false prophet had been thrown. They will be tormented day and night for ever and ever.' Revelation 20:7-10

Why was satan set free once more?
We are not given a reason in the book of Revelation for satan being spared for the thousand years, or why he should be released; nor are we given any reason why those who live under Christ's rule on earth can again be deceived. Perhaps his release was to test the hearts of men who still bore the mark of sinful nature; Man lost the potential for obedience in the garden of Eden, and is fatally flawed ever since.

However: we need not speculate

'Therefore, son of man, prophesy and say to Gog: This is what the Sovereign Lord says: In that day, when my people Israel are living in safety, will you not take notice of it? You will come from your place in the far north, you and many nations with you, all of them riding on horses, a great hoard, a mighty army. You will advance against my people Israel like a cloud that covers the land. In days to come Gog, I will bring you against my land, so that the nations may know me when I show myself holy through you before their eyes. This is what the Sovereign Lord says: Are you not the one I spoke of in former days by my servants the prophets of Israel? At that time they prophesied for years that I would bring you against them. This is what will happen in that day: when Gog attacks the land of Israel, my hot anger will be aroused, declares the Sovereign Lord.' Ezekiel 38:14-19

The reason satan was released again was to fulfil God's word.

'...In the latter days I will bring you against my land, that the nations may know me, when through you O Gog, I vindicate my holiness before their eyes.' Ezekiel 38:16 RSV

God said he would bring satan against Israel when they were living securely - so He had to do it. He cast satan into the lake of fire where the beast and the false prophet were thrown.

'How you have fallen from heaven, O morning star, son of the dawn! You have been cast down to the earth, you once laid low the nations! You said in your heart, "I will ascend to heaven; I will raise my throne above the stars of God; I will sit enthroned on the mount of assembly, on the utmost heights of the sacred mountain I will ascend above the tops of the clouds; I will make myself like the most high." But you are brought down to the grave, to the depths of the pit.' Isaiah 14:12-15

CHAPTER 13

The Second Resurrection
The Last Judgement

At this time satan has been thrown into the lake of burning sulphur, where the beast out of the sea and the false prophet were thrown. The thousand years of Christ's reign on earth, when time is still measured, ends; the last day has dawned; the day of judgement; the day before we enter eternity arrives.

Paul gives us an insight into what takes place.
"According to the Lord's own word, we tell you that we who are still alive, who are left till the coming of the Lord, will certainly not precede those who have fallen asleep. For the Lord himself will come down from heaven, with a loud command, with the trumpet call of God, and the dead in Christ will rise first. After that, we who are still alive and are left will be caught up together with them in the clouds to meet the Lord in the air. And so we will be with the Lord forever.' 2 Thessalonians 4:15-16

All who know and love the Lord are gathered to meet with the Lord in the air, resurrected, made alive, raised body and soul. This includes the Jews who died during the Lord's earthly reign; then those Jews who are alive and left at the trumpet call of God.

But what about the rest of mankind?
'When the thousand years are over, satan will be released from his prison and will go out to deceive the nations in the four corners of the earth -

Gog and Magog - to gather them for battle. In number they are like the sand on the seashore. They marched across the breadth of the earth and surrounded the camp of God's people, the city he loves. But fire came down from heaven and devoured them.' Revelation 20:7-9

'I will send fire on Magog and on those who live in safety in the coast lands, and they will know that I am the Lord.' Ezekiel 39:6

The Dead are Judged by God Almighty

'Then I saw a great white throne and him who was seated on it. Earth and sky fled from his presence, and there was no place for them. And I saw the dead, great and small, standing before the throne, and books were opened. Another book was opened, which was the book of life. The dead were judged according to what they had done as recorded in the books. The sea gave up the dead that were in it, and Death and Hades gave up the dead that were in them, and each person was judged according to what they had done. Then Death and Hades were thrown into the lake of fire. The lake of fire is the second death. If anyone's name was not found written in the book of life, he was thrown into the lake of fire.' Revelation 20:11-15

No explanation is needed as to who the judge is, or who is to be judged. "I saw the dead, great and small, standing before the throne". All are resurrected, made alive, body and soul. All are judged according to what is recorded in the books, including the book of life: all except those judged at the first resurrection. But you might ask, "Why are there three places that give up the dead: The sea, Hades, and Death?" I confess, I can only speculate about the sea. I believe the sea is mentioned because those lost at sea are not accounted for; there is no visible evidence that they died. This would include all who died with no known knowledge of their death. However, they are accounted for in Hades and Death; only these are thrown into the lake of fire.

How do we know that when people die they go to two different places? Consider what Jesus said to John before He gave him the Revelation of what was to come.

'When I saw Him, I fell at his feet as though dead. Then he placed his right hand on me and said: "Do not be afraid. I am the Living One; I was dead, and behold I am alive for ever and ever! And I hold the Keys of Death and Hades." Revelation 1:17-18

'and Death and Hades gave up the dead that were in them.' Revelation 20:13

And we have this parable Jesus told
'There was a rich man who was dressed in purple and fine linen and lived in luxury every day. At his gate was laid a beggar named Lazarus, covered with sores and longing to eat what fell from the rich man's table. Even the dogs came and licked his sores. The time came when the beggar died and the angels carried him to Abraham's side. The rich man also died and was buried. In hell, where he was in torment, he looked up and saw Abraham far away, with Lazarus by his side. So he called to him, "Father Abraham, have pity on me and send Lazarus to dip the tip of his finger in water and cool my tongue, because I am in agony in this fire. But Abraham replied "Son, remember that in your lifetime you received your good things, while Lazarus received bad things, but now he is comforted here and you are in agony. And besides all this, between us and you a great chasm has been fixed, so those who want to go from here to you cannot, nor can anyone cross over from there to us." Luke 16:19-26

When we die, the righteous and the unrighteous go to different places. One place that is called hell, and the other a place of comfort. We can note the difference in the departure; one carried off by angels; the other buried. But what is the difference between Hades and Death? There is a great difference according to the Scriptures.

The Lord says that Hades is the place called hell
'Simon Peter answered, "You are the Christ, the Son of the living God." Jesus replied, "Blessed are you son of Jonah, for this was not revealed to you by man, but by my Father in heaven. And I tell you that you are Peter, and on this rock I will build my church, and the gates of Hades will not overcome it." Matthew 16:16

Above we have from the Lord himself a description of hell, a place of fire and torment, and agony.

But death is a place of comfort and rest

*'Then the Lord appeared at the Tent in a pillar of cloud, and the cloud stood over the entrance to the tent. And the Lord said to Moses: "**You are going to rest** with your fathers, and these people will soon prostitute themselves to the foreign gods of the land they are entering.'* Deuteronomy 3:15-16

*'As for you (Daniel) go your way till the end. **You will rest**, and then at the end of the days you will rise to receive your allotted inheritance."* Daniel 12:13

That's all right for Moses and Daniel, but what about the rest of God's people?

*'The righteous perish, and no one ponders it in his heart; devout men are taken away, and no one understands that the righteous are taken away to be spared from evil. Those who walk uprightly enter into peace; **they find rest** as they lie in death.'* Isaiah 57:1-2

Death is a place of rest and comfort, where the righteous await the coming of the Lord, when their souls are raised from the first death; clothed in fine white linen, like the souls under the altar, they ride out with the armies of heaven. And after the thousand years of the Lord's reign on earth ends, they are made alive, raised body and soul for judgement at the second resurrection. They are raised up; united with their new bodies on the last day, and each judged according to what they had done, as recorded in the books, and the book of life. Then Death and Hades, no longer needed, are thrown into the lake of fire. 'The lake of fire is the second death. If anyone's name was not found written in the book of life, he was thrown into the lake of fire, where the devil, the beast, and the false prophet had been thrown, where they will be tormented day and night for ever and ever."

The New Jerusalem

'Then I saw a new heaven and a new earth, for the first heaven and the first earth had passed away, and there was no longer any sea. I saw the Holy City, the new Jerusalem, coming down out of heaven from God, prepared as a bride beautifully dressed for her husband. And I heard a loud voice from the throne saying, "Now the dwelling of God is with men, and he will live with them. They will be his people, and God himself will be with them and be their God. He will wipe every tear from their eyes. There will be no more death or mourning or crying or pain, for the old order of things have passed away." He who was seated on the throne said, "I am making everything new!" Then he said, "write this down, for these words are trustworthy and true." He said to me: "It is done. I am the Alpha and the Omega, the beginning and the end..." Revelation 21:1-6

'Then he told me, "Do not seal up the words of the prophecy of this book, because the time is near." Revelation 22 :10

CHAPTER 14

The Riddle of the Kings | The Scarlet Beast

The object of my study is to put in order the events of what would come later in the Revelation given to John. Having done so, the question arises: How do you know you have got it right? I take some confidence from the table of events, that shows at a glance, the parallel events, and how the sequence of events unfold as we read across the table. However, it is not left to me to decide if I got it right, for we are given a riddle to solve that requires a clear understanding of the Revelation. The riddle is two-fold: who or what does the scarlet beast represent? And who are the kings in the riddle we are given?

'Then the angel carried me away in the Spirit into a desert. There I saw a woman sitting on a scarlet beast that was covered with blasphemous names and had seven heads and ten horns.' Revelation 17:3

'The beast, which you saw, once was, now is not, and will come up out of the Abyss and go to his destruction. The inhabitants of the earth whose names have not been written in the book of life from the creation of the world will be astonished when they see the beast, because he once was, now is not, and yet will come.' Revelation 17:8

We know from our study, the beast with seven heads and ten horns is the northern kingdom, and kingdoms have kings. The seven heads are seven kings. This is the bringing together of all the northern kings, from the opening of the first seal to the coming of the man of lawlessness, and the finality of their purpose, a satanic world kingdom. A kingdom that has the beast that comes up from the Abyss for its king, who leads the whole rebellious world to war against the King of kings and the Lord of lords. This is a kingdom that was and rises again before the Lord's second coming: a satanic kingdom, the scarlet beast, that the woman is seated on at a place of seven hills.

Now to test our understanding of all this (the study so far) we are given a riddle

'This calls for a mind with wisdom. The seven heads are seven hills on which the woman sits. They are also seven kings. Five have fallen, one is, the other has not yet come; but when he does come, he must remain for a little while. The beast who once was, and now is not, is an eighth king. He belongs to the seven and is going to his destruction.' Revelation 17:9-11

Having completed the study of the kings and kingdoms, we should be able to answer this riddle. We know this beast with seven heads is the northern kingdom, and the fourth of Daniel's four kingdoms, and has the king we know to be the contemptible person: the beast out of the sea; the last and seventh earthly king of the North. Five are fallen, one remains, the other has not come. So according to the riddle, we are in the time of the sixth king. From our study we know that the king mentioned before the contemptible person was the king of the third seal, the "tax collector," who was given authority to represent the kings of the divided northern kingdom. Why are we given this king to count from? It is with him we reach the end of the beginning, and with the next king we reach the beginning of the end. We are about to turn to the other side of the scroll, and enter the last seven years, the last week of years, of the Feast of Weeks.

So who are the five kings before him - The Tax Collector - who have fallen?

'Now then I tell you the truth: three more kings will appear in Persia, and then a fourth, who will be far richer than all the others. When he has *gained power by his wealth, he will stir up everyone against the kingdom of Greece. Then a mighty king will appear who will rule with great power and do as he pleases.'* Daniel 11:2-3

During the time the king of Persia is building the southern kingdom to become the king of the South, the northern kingdom exists and has a king. After this king comes a mighty king who will rule with great power and do as he pleases. He is the second king of the North, counting from the time the king of Persia rides out.

So who are the five fallen kings, and the two that make the seventh and eighth?

We have the king of the North who ruled when the southern kingdom was being established.

Then we have the mighty king who will do as he pleases.

The northern kingdom is dived into four, with four kings, one of which is our tax-collector king who represents the whole of the northern kingdom, and he is counted as the sixth king.

Then a contemptible person, the beast out of the sea who has not been given the honour of royalty, unites the northern kingdom, giving us the seventh king.

But what about the eighth, who belongs to the seven?

From our study we know that satan rules the world in the last three and a half years before the Lord returns; a king of the north, who belongs to the seven, the ultimate ruler of the northern kingdom.

Then we have the ten horns - Who are they?

'Then I saw three evil spirits that looked like frogs; they came out of the mouth of the dragon, out of the mouth of the beast and out of the mouth of the false prophet. They are spirits of demons performing miraculous signs, and they go out to the kings of the whole world, to gather them for the battle on the great day of God Almighty. - Then they gathered the kings together to the place that in Hebrew is called Armageddon.' Revelation 16:13-14; 16:16

'The ten horns you saw are ten kings who have not yet received a kingdom, but who for one hour will receive authority as kings along with the beast. They have one purpose and will give their power and authority to the beast. They will make war against the Lamb, but the Lamb will overcome them because he is Lord of lords and King of kings - and with him will be his called, chosen and faithful followers.' Revelation 17:12-14

The ten kings of the earth, who represent the remainder of the rebellious world at Armageddon; deceived by satan into making war against the King of kings and the Lord of lords. This leaves one more part of the riddle to solve: the place of seven hills where the woman sits.

'There I saw a woman sitting on a scarlet beast that was covered with blasphemous names and had seven heads and ten horns. Revelation 17:3

'The beast which you saw, once was, now is not, and will come up out of the Abyss and go to his destruction. And when he comes up out of the Abyss the inhabitants of the earth whose names have not been written in the book of life, from the creation of the world will be astonished, because he once was, now is not, and yet will come. This calls for a mind with wisdom. The seven heads are seven hills on which the woman sits.' Revelation 17:8-9

We know from our study that the scarlet beast is the northern kingdom, Daniel's fourth beast; the rise of the "Roman Empire" again; an empire which was, is not, and has come up out of the Abyss. A kingdom whose geographical area and power is similar to the former Roman Empire, with a king who has been given satanic powers to do satan's will. A kingdom that will be ruled by satan in its last few years. The Roman Empire was the world power when the Lord came to save the world from sin; raised a second time before His return and given power over all the peoples of the earth. However, the political power base of this risen again empire is not Rome. It looks like the

Roman Empire; but where is the seat of power? Who knows? The first reference to the king of the North is the king of Greece. However, we are now directed to the former imperial city of Rome where the woman (Babylon the Great - The Mother of Prostitutes) sits.

Conclusion

Having completed my study of the Book of Revelation, I look back with a sense of wonder at how the Lord led me step by step to unravel the order of events leading to His second coming, and at the reason revealed by putting these events in order. A logical revelation from the Scriptures that removes all the controversy, and answers many of the questions we may have about the Lord's coming and the end times.

The object of the study is to share with others God's plan for bringing His creation, the world, to its end, and its people to judgement, and the fulfilment of His eternal purpose. That is, the part He has for His chosen people, the Israelites, to play in bringing His people, Jew and Christian, to eternal fellowship with Him, and add to what Christians know, and believe, about the events before and after the Lord's second coming.

Such is the content of the book, and how the Scriptures are used to reveal the order of events, that I believe it necessary to include all the relevant Scriptures in the book. And it is my prayer that the subject of the book will attract readers from all walks of life; perhaps some not in possession of their own Bible, to be encouraged by God's Word in the book, to purchase a Bible and read it; for His Word reveals mankind's greatest need, and how it can be satisfied in the Lord Jesus Christ.

If there is one enduring trait of mankind, it is to know what the future holds. From the Bible we can learn the true purpose of life, and how and why we came to be. From the same source, God's Word, we can know for certain what the eternal future is for each one of us, for He has revealed it to us in His Word.

PART THREE

Appendices and the Table of Events

APPENDIX 1

Supplementary Study Table

The Seven Feasts of Jehovah - God's plan for the Redemption of Israel

Leviticus 23:1-36

THE SEVEN FEASTS OF JEHOVAH	RELATED EVENTS
The Lord's Passover The Feast of Unleavened Bread	
	Christ Crucified Present age - Feast of Harvest
To be fulfilled	*To be fulfilled*
The Feast of Weeks	
	Firstfruits of Israel - New grain presented to God Feast of Ingathering - Christians gathered from the earth
The Feast of Trumpets The Day of Atonement The Feast of Tabernacles	Messiah returns Messiahs 1,000 year reign begins The first resurrection
The Feast of Tabernacles ends The Sabbath	Messiah's 1,000 year reign ends The second resurrection God Almighty judges all Eternity

Supplementary Study to the Revelation of Events

The Seven Feasts of Jehovah

The seven Feasts of Jehovah are the steps to be taken by God's chosen people, Israel, on their journey to the Promised Land. They foretell what is to take place in God's calendar of redemption for the Jews; starting with the Lord's Passover and coming to their completeness at the Closing Assembly. In a similar way God foretold salvation for the Gentiles, entwined as it is with the redemption of the Israelites.

The seven Feasts of Jehovah are for the Israelites Sacred Assemblies: Leviticus 23
The Sabbath - The Lord's Passover - The Feast of Unleavened Bread - The Feast of Weeks - The Feast of Trumpets - The day of Atonement - The Feast of Tabernacles

In the book of Genesis we are given the first indication that God would provide a Saviour
'So the Lord God said to the serpent, "Because you have done this, cursed are you above all the livestock and all the wild animals! You will crawl on your belly and you will eat dust all the days of your life. And I will put enmity between you and the woman, and between your offspring and hers: He will crush your head, and you will strike his heel." Genesis 3:14-15

In the book of Exodus God gives us three feasts that foretell those the Saviour would save
'Three times a year you are to celebrate a festival to me. Celebrate the feast of Unleavened Bread; for seven days eat bread made without yeast, as I

command you. Do this at the appointed time in the month of Abib, for in that month you came out of Egypt. "No one is to appear before me empty handed. "Celebrate the feast of Harvest with the first fruits of the crops you sow in your field. "Celebrate the Feast of Ingathering at the end of the year, when you gather in your crops from the field.' Exodus 23:14-16

In Deuteronomy God gives us three annual feasts that foretell the redemption of the Israelites

'Three times a year all your men must appear before the Lord your God at the place he will choose; at the Feast of Unleavened Bread, the Feast of Weeks and the Feast of Tabernacles. No man should appear before the Lord empty-handed. Each of you must bring a gift in proportion to the way the Lord your God has blessed you.' Deuteronomy 16:16

We have to ask: why were two sets of three feasts given by the Lord, each beginning with the Feast of Unleavened Bread? Why is the first set of feasts inclusive: no one is to appear before me empty handed; and the second set exclusive: all your men must appear before the Lord? Why does one of the sets have three of the Feasts of Jehovah that are for the Israelites sacred assemblies, and the other set, although given to the Israelites, have two feasts that are not Feasts of Jehovah? Is it because the two sets of feasts are meant for two groups of people? The Lord's Passover Feast was not included because both sets of feasts looked forward to a time after what was foretold had come.
Let us test this hypothesis.

The Passover Feast and the Feast of Unleavened Bread

'The Lord said to Moses and Aaron in Egypt, "This month is to be for you the first month, the first month of your year. Tell the whole community of Israel that on the tenth day of this month each man is to take a lamb for his family, one for each household. If any household is to small for a whole lamb, they must share one with their nearest neighbour, having taken into account the number of people there are. You are to determine the amount of lamb needed in accordance with what each person will eat. The animals

you choose must be year-old males without defect, and you may take them from the sheep or the goats. Take care of them until the fourteenth day of the month, when all the people of the community of Israel must slaughter them at twilight. Then they are to take some of the blood and put it on the sides and tops of the door frames of the houses where they eat the lambs. That same night they are to eat the meat roasted over fire, along with bitter herbs, and bread made without yeast. Do not eat the meat raw or cooked in water, but roast it over fire - head, legs and inner parts. Do not leave any of it till morning; if some is left till morning, you must burn it. This is how you are to eat it: with your cloak tucked into your belt, your sandals on your feet and your staff in your hand. Eat it in haste; it is the Lord's Passover. On the same night I will pass through Egypt and strike down every first born - both men and animals - and I will bring judgement on all the gods of Egypt. I am the Lord. The blood will be a sign for you on the houses where you are; and when I see the blood, I will pass over you. No destructive plague will touch you when I strike Egypt. This is the day you are to commemorate; for generations to come you shall celebrate it as a festival to the Lord - a lasting ordinance. For seven days you are to eat bread made without yeast. On the first day remove the yeast from your houses, for whoever eats anything with yeast in it from the first day through the seventh must be cut off from Israel. On the first day hold a sacred assembly, and another on the seventh day. Do no work at all on these days, except to prepare food for everyone to eat - that is all you may do.' Exodus 12:1-15

The Lord's Passover Feast was only to be celebrated by Jews, and those who became Jews

'The Lord said to Moses and Aaron, "These are the regulations for the Passover: "No foreigner is to eat of it. Any slave you have bought may eat of it after you have circumcised him, but a temporary resident and a hired worker may not eat of it. "It must be eaten inside one house, take none of the meat outside the house. Do not break any of the bones. The whole community of Israel must celebrate it. An alien living among you who wants to celebrate the Lord's Passover must have all the males in his household circumcised; then he may take part like one born in the land.

No uncircumcised male may eat of it. The same law applies to the native born and to the alien living among you." Exodus 12:43-49

The Passover Feast and the Feast of Unleavened Bread are followed by two ordinances that are linked together by reference to the same wave-sheaf, but separate in their application. In the first, the Lord ordains the Feast of Harvest; in the second, the Feast of Weeks, the next feast in the sequence of the Feasts of Jehovah. (Leviticus 23:1– 44) It is clear that these ordinances are for two groups of people, as the second can only apply to Jews.

The Lord ordains the Feast of Harvest
The first ordinance: The Feast of Unleavened Bread; the Feast of Harvest; The Feast of Ingathering
'The Lord said to Moses, "Speak to the Israelites and say to them: When you enter the land I am going to give you and you reap it's harvest, bring to the priest a sheaf of the first grain you harvest. He is to wave the sheaf before the Lord so it will be accepted on your behalf: the priest is to wave it on the day after the Sabbath. On the day you wave the sheaf, you must sacrifice as a burnt offering to the Lord a lamb a year old without defect, together with it's grain offering of two tenths of an ephah of fine flour mixed with oil - an offering made to the Lord by fire a pleasing aroma - and its drink offering of a quarter of a hin of wine. You must not eat any bread, or roasted or new grain, until the very day you bring this offering to your God. This is to be a lasting ordinance for the generations to come, wherever you live.' Leviticus 23:9-14 NIRV

Why was the Lord's Passover Feast not appointed when the first set of feasts were given? These feasts looked forward to the time after the Passover was fulfilled; what was foretold took place: Christ came, the Lamb of God was sacrificed. These feasts are for those who would have no part in the celebration of the Passover Feast, and given to the Israelites, to hold in trust for those foretold by them; those who would believe in Jesus' death for their sin. Their journey to the promised land begins at Calvary; their Lamb has been sacrificed, and for the rest of their lives they are to celebrate the Feast of Unleavened bread by living holy lives. Leaven is used here to depict evil, i.e. sin. Bread without leaven represents lives without sin. The Feast of Unleavened Bread was and is a call for all God's people, Jew and Christian, to live lives that are holy. Thus one could say: as we need daily bread, we are to observe this call to holiness daily. The Feast of Unleavened Bread is an ongoing feast for Jew and Gentile.

The wave-sheaf, the first of the firstfruits is accepted by God on behalf of the Gentiles and Jews, but only appropriated by those who put their trust in the blood of the lamb that was slain. They are the recipients of what was foretold by the Passover Feast. They celebrate the Feast of Unleavened Bread and the Feast of Harvest with the Lamb and the bread made without yeast, the bread from the first of the firstfruits, and the wine. From our perspective, the Lamb has been sacrificed at Calvary; the Feast of Harvest begins, and we celebrate with the bread and the wine, symbols of the Lord's body and blood, until the Feast of Ingathering when the full number of Christians will be made complete. (The harvest of the earth: Rev.14:14-20) From this set of feasts and its ordinance we have the first mention of those the Saviour would save, and the foundation on which the Lord's Supper stands. But with Israel the shadow remains: because of their unbelief they continue to celebrate the Passover; they reject the lamb that was slain at Calvary; they wait for Messiah, their Deliverer from Zion.

Israel waits for the number of the Gentiles to be complete, and their deliverer from Zion

'I do not want you to be ignorant of this mystery, brothers, so that you may not be conceited: Israel has experienced a hardening in part until the full number of the Gentiles has come in. And so all Israel will be saved, as it is written. "The deliverer will come from Zion: he will turn Godlessness away from Jacob. And this is my covenant with them when I take away their sins." Romans 11:25-27

Israel waits for the Feast of Ingathering, when the earth will be harvested, and the full number of Christians are gathered. Then Messiah will come, and the remnant of Israel will be saved. Jew and Gentile, in this present age, share in the Feast of Unleavened Bread and celebrate the Feast of Harvest. But the Feast of Harvest and the Feast of Ingathering were not included in the Seven Feasts of Jehovah given to the Israelites as sacred assemblies.

The fact remains, they were given these two feasts, and to observe with those feasts decreed for Jews
'Celebrate the Feast of weeks with the firstfruits of the wheat harvest, and the Feast of Ingathering at the turn of the year.' Exodus 34:22

The Lord ordains the Feast of Weeks
The second ordinance: The Feast of Unleavened Bread – the Feast of Weeks – the Feast of Tabernacles
'From the day after the Sabbath, the day you brought the wave offering, count of seven full weeks. Count off fifty days up to the day after the seventh Sabbath, and then present an offering of new grain to the Lord. From wherever you live, bring two loaves made of two-tenths of an ephah of fine flour, baked with yeast, as a wave offering of firstfruits to the Lord. Present with this bread seven male lambs, each a year old and without defect, one young bull and two rams. They will be a burnt offering to the Lord. Then sacrifice one male goat for a sin offering and two lambs, each a year old, for a fellowship offering. The priest is to wave the two lambs before the Lord as a wave offering, together with the bread of the firstfruits. They are a sacred offering to the Lord for the priest. On that same day you are to proclaim a sacred assembly and do no regular work. This is to be a lasting ordinance for the generations to come, wherever you live.' Leviticus.23:15-18

The Feast of Weeks is given in Leviticus 23:15-21, as is the outworking of the Feast of Weeks
'Count of seven Sabbaths of years - seven times seven years - so that the

seven Sabbaths of years amount to a period of forty-nine years. Then have the trumpet sounded everywhere on the tenth day of the seventh month; on the Day of Atonement, sound the trumpet throughout the land. Consecrate the fiftieth year and proclaim liberty through out the land to all it's inhabitants. It shall be a jubilee for you.' Leviticus 25:8-10

Daniel brings together the forty-nine years (seven times seven) with seventy sevens decreed for the Israelites

'Seventy "sevens" are decreed for your people and your holy city to finish transgression, to put an end to sin, to atone for wickedness, to bring in everlasting righteousness, to seal up prophecy and anoint the Most Holy. Know and understand this: from the issuing of the decree to restore and rebuild Jerusalem until the Anointed One, the ruler, comes there will be seven "sevens" and sixty-two "sevens." It will be rebuilt with streets and a trench, but in times of trouble. After sixty-two "sevens" the Anointed One will be cut off and will have nothing. The people of the ruler who will come will destroy the city and the sanctuary. The end will come like a flood: War will continue to the end, and desolations have been decreed. He will confirm a covenant with many for one "seven." In the middle of the "seven" he will put an end to sacrifice and offering. And on a wing of the temple he will set up an abomination that causes desolation, until the end that is decreed is poured out on him.' Daniel 9:24 -27

The mystery revealed to prophets

These verses foretell the first and the second coming of our Lord, and when He would come. The same context foretells the coming of satan who causes desolation, until the end that is decreed is poured out on him. (See - The Rebellion against God -The Rule of satan Begins - The Riddle of the Kings chapter 10). However, our interest is in the coming of the Lord. The first time after sixty-two "sevens", He would be cut off and have nothing, as far as the Israelites are concerned.

'He was in the world, and though the world was made through him, the world did not recognise him. He came to that which was his own, but his

own did not receive him. Yet to all who received him, to those who believed in his name he gave the right to become children of God.' John 1:10

Jesus' death at Calvary begins the Feast of Harvest, generally known as the Days of Grace. This is the interval between the sixty-two "sevens" and the seven "sevens" that continues until the Feast of Ingathering ends with the Harvest of the Earth, when those who know and love the Lord will be harvested to make their number complete.

So what is the purpose of His second coming?

'For Christ did not enter a man-made sanctuary that was only a copy of the true one; he entered heaven itself, now to appear for us in God's presence. Nor did he enter heaven to offer himself again and again, the way the high priest enters the Most Holy Place every year with the blood that is not his own. Then Christ would have to suffer many times since the creation of the world. But now he has appeared once for all at the end of the ages to do away with sin by the sacrifice of himself. Just as man is destined to die once, and after that to face judgement, so Christ was sacrificed once to take away the sins of many people; and he will appear a second time, not to bear sin, but to bring salvation to those who are waiting for him.' Hebrews 9:24-28

The Lord Jesus Christ came the first time and was sacrificed to take away the sins of many people, and appears a second time, not to bear sin, **but to bring salvation to those who wait for Him.** Who are waiting for salvation? Not the Christians who have been harvested at the Feast of Ingathering, or the Gentiles who remain and refuse to repent, but the next crop to be harvested, the remnant of the Israelites who wait for Messiah their Kinsman Redeemer. But before the Lord's return, the Israelites were to celebrate the Feast of Weeks with the firstfruits of the wheat harvest.

"Celebrate the Feast of Weeks with the firstfruits of the wheat harvest, and the Feast of Ingathering at the turn of the year.' Exodus 34:22

'From the day after the Sabbath, the day you brought the wave offering, count of seven full weeks. Count off fifty days up to the day after the seventh Sabbath, and then present an offering of new grain to the Lord. From wherever you live, bring two loaves made of two-tenths of an ephah of fine flour, baked with yeast, as a wave offering of firstfruits to the Lord.'
Leviticus.23:15-18

The wave-sheaf, the first of the firstfruits, their Kinsman Redeemer, has been accepted by God. Now from this same crop must come the rest of the firstfruits before the main harvest begins. As one of the offerings of the second ordinance, the priest was to wave two lambs as a wave offering before the Lord, foretelling that the Lord would come to earth twice before Israel's redemption. Together with the two lambs, an offering of new grain was to be made to the Lord, as two loaves baked with yeast, the bread of the firstfruits. When Paul writes: 'Israel has experienced a hardening in part until the full number of the Gentiles has come in,' he is saying that not all Israel has been hardened. Therefore there are some within Israel who are to be found blameless in God's sight. These are the firstfruits of the twelve tribes of Israel.

Then I heard the number of those who were sealed:144,000 from all the tribes of Israel.' Revelation.7:4

'Then I looked, and there before me was the Lamb, standing on mount Zion, and with him 144,000 who had his name and his Father's name written on their foreheads. And I heard a sound from heaven like the roar of rushing waters and like a loud peal of thunder. The sound I heard was like that of harpists playing their harps. And they sang a new song before the throne and before the four living creatures and the elders. No one could learn the song except the 144,000 who were redeemed from the earth. These are those who did not defile themselves with women, for they kept themselves pure. They follow the Lamb wherever he goes. They were purchased from among men and offered as firstfruits to God

and the Lamb. No lie was found in their mouths; they are blameless.'
Revelation 14:1-5

Today the Jews wait for the last week of years of the Feast of Weeks
to begin; then when fifty days have passed, the firstfruits will be
redeemed from the earth. This will be followed by the beginning
of the Feast of Ingathering at the turn of the year: the harvest of
the elect, their number made complete at the Harvest of the Earth.
Meanwhile the Feast of Weeks continues until the Feast of Trumpets;
the second time the Lord comes at the end of the forty-nine years that
is also the end of the sixty-ninth week of years of the seventy weeks.
The final seven years of the seventy "sevens" decreed for the children
of Israel and their holy city is for the rebuilding of Jerusalem that
satan will destroy.

The Feast of Trumpets - Messiah comes to bring salvation to those who are waiting

'The Lord said to Moses, "Say to the Israelites: On the first day of the seventh month you are to have a day of rest, a sacred assembly commemorated with trumpet blasts. Do no regular work, but present an offering made to the Lord by fire." Leviticus 23:23-25

The Feast of Weeks ends with the Feast of Trumpets. What better
way to welcome Messiah; a Feast of Trumpets to herald His coming
to reign!

Now is the time to bring in everlasting righteousness

"Seventy sevens are decreed for your people and your holy city to finish transgression to put an end to sin, to atone for wickedness, to bring in everlasting righteousness, to seal up vision and prophecy, and to anoint the Most Holy.' Daniel 9:24

'On that day I will set out to destroy all the nations that attack Jerusalem. And I will pour out on the house of David and the inhabitants of

Jerusalem the Spirit of grace and supplication. They will look on me the one they pierced, and they will mourn for him as one mourns for an only child, and grieve bitterly for him as one grieves for a first-born son.' Zechariah 12:9-10

Messiahs return brings the Day of Atonement

'The Lord said to Moses, "The tenth day of this seventh month is the Day of Atonement. Hold a sacred assembly and deny yourselves, and present an offering made to the Lord by fire. Do no work on that day, because it is the Day of Atonement, when atonement is made for you before the Lord your God." Leviticus 23:26-28

"On that day a fountain will be opened to the house of David and the inhabitants of Jerusalem, to cleanse them from sin and impurity. "On that day, I will banish the names of idols from the land, and they will be remembered no more," declares the Lord Almighty. "I will remove both the prophets and the spirit of impurity from the land.' Zechariah 13:1-2

The Feast of Tabernacles - Christ's thousand-year reign on earth begins

'The Lord said to Moses, "Say to the Israelites: On the fifteenth day of the seventh month the Lord's Feast of Tabernacles begins, and it lasts for seven days. The first day is a sacred assembly; do no regular work. For seven days present offerings made to the Lord by fire, and on the eighth day hold a sacred assembly and present an offering made to the Lord by fire. It is the closing assembly; do no regular work.' Leviticus 23:33-36

'So beginning with the fifteenth day of the seventh month, after you have gathered the crops of the land, celebrate the festival to the Lord for seven days; the first day is a day of rest, and the eighth day also is a day of rest. On the first day you are to take choice fruit from the trees, and palm fronds, leafy branches and poplars, and rejoice before the Lord your God for seven days. Celebrate this as a festival to the Lord for seven days each year. This is to be a lasting ordinance for the generations to come: celebrate

it in the seventh month. Live in booths for seven days: All native born Israelites are to live in booths so your descendants will know that I had the Israelites live in booths when I brought them out of Egypt. I am the Lord your God.' Leviticus 23:39-43

The crops are gathered – the Feast of Tabernacles is celebrated year after year for a thousand years
'Then the survivors from all the nations that have attacked Jerusalem will go up year after year to worship the King, the Lord Almighty, and to celebrate the Feast of Tabernacles.' Zechariah 14:16

The Feast of Tabernacles ends; the thousand years are over; the Closing Assembly; the eighth day of the feast
Is the last day, the day of judgement, the Closing Assembly? No! because the Closing Assembly is a Sacred Assembly, the first day of the Sabbath, which is for God's people the beginning of eternity: Jews redeemed by the Grace of God, and Christians by the Blood of Christ.

I began this part of the study by suggesting that the two groups of feasts starting with the Feast of Unleavened Bread were meant for two groups of people, and looked forward to a time after the Lord's death at Calvary and His return at Armageddon.

(1) The Feast of Unleavened Bread; the Feast of Harvest; the Feast of Ingathering
(2) The Feast of Unleavened Bread; the Feast of Weeks; the Feast of Tabernacles

The Passover Feast is fulfilled by the Lord's death at Calvary, leaving the Feast of Unleavened Bread to be celebrated by both Jew and Christian. The Feast of Harvest begins at Calvary and is followed by the beginning of the Feast of Weeks that is celebrated with the firstfruits of the wheat harvest, the resurrection of 144,000 Jews, and the Feast of Ingathering at the turn of the year; the completion of the barley harvest; the harvest of the Elect, their number made complete at the Harvest of the Earth. The Feast of Weeks continues until the Feast of Trumpets, when the Lord returns and the Day of Atonement takes place. This leaves the Feast of Unleavened Bread and the Feast of Tabernacles to be celebrated for the thousand years of the Lord's reign on earth, until the Father Almighty comes at the end of the age to judge the earth.

APPENDIX 3

Comments on Chapter 10

The Harvest of the Earth

The Coming of the Almighty - The Judge of all the Earth

A friend and brother in the Lord asked me to consider some verses of Scripture that seem to cast doubt on there being a "harvest" of Christians, to complete their number, before Messiah returns for the redemption of the Jews, and to reign on earth for 1,000 years. Clearly there would be no Christians left on earth at His return.

These are the verses

'Brothers we do not want you to be ignorant about those who fall asleep, or to grieve like the rest of men, who have no hope. We believe that Jesus died and rose again and so we believe that God will bring with Jesus those who have fallen asleep in him. According to the Lord's own word, we tell you that we who are still alive, who are left till the coming of the Lord, will certainly not precede those who have fallen asleep. For the lord himself will come down from heaven, with a loud command, with the voice of the archangel and with the trumpet call of God, and the dead in Christ will rise first. After that, we who are left will be caught up together with them in the clouds to meet the Lord in the air. And so we will be with the Lord forever. Therefore encourage each other with these words.'
1 Thessalonians 4:13-18

The doubt is raised by the commonly held belief that there will be Christians alive at the Lord's return, and the verses we are considering is His second coming. To help us understand, we need to know who Paul is responding to in these verses. A first reading of Paul's letter to the Thessalonians is enough to show he is inclusive in language and tone because he is addressing both Jew and Greek Christians. Paul was writing to the whole church, but it is evident from the letter that there were groups within it. This raises the question: to which group did Paul send the letter with the command that it be read to the whole church? I believe Paul is addressing questions that can only apply to Jews, and therefore sends the letter to them.

This finds some support, in that Paul, knowing how Jews thought about Gentiles, writes
'I charge you before the Lord to have this letter read to all the brothers.' 1 Thessalonians 5:27

Some translations of this verse use the word "adjure". This would command under solemn oath. Paul is concerned that the Jews will not include the Greeks, so he charges them, before the Lord, to read the letter to all the brothers.

And we get an insight into some of the difficulties between the brothers
'Now we ask you brothers, to respect those who work hard among you, who are over you in the Lord and who admonish you. Hold them in the highest regard in love because of their work. Live in peace with one another.' 1 Thessalonians 5:12-13

If we say these verses refer to the coming of Messiah, we must ask the question: how can this be? The text of the verses we are considering show clearly that this is the last day, which is the day of judgement, the day before we enter eternity. And according to the book of Revelation this would be the second resurrection, when all are raised body and soul; made alive for judgement. So when does the first resurrection, the resurrection of those who came out of the great tribulation, take place? When does the thousand years of Christ's reign on earth begin?

Born king of the Jews (Isaiah 9:7); Crucified, King of the Jews (Matthew 27:37); Yet to reign over them

'The Lord will be king over the whole earth. On that day there will be one Lord, and his name the only name.' Zechariah 14:9

How can there be survivors? - When messiah comes to redeem the Israelites

'And the angel saw the sorrow of those of the House of David and of the inhabitants of Jerusalem, the remnants of Israel; for the Lord poured out on them a spirit of grace and supplication. They looked on Him the one they had pierced, and mourned for Him as one mourns for an only child, and grieved bitterly for Him as one grieves for a first born son.' Zechariah 12:10

Messiah, who their forefathers rejected, has come, Lord and King over the whole earth, and His name the only Name.

'Then the survivors from all the nations that have attacked Jerusalem will go up year after year to worship the King, the Lord almighty, and to celebrate the Feast of Tabernacles.' Zechariah 14:16

Messiahs reign on earth ends - The Feast of Tabernacles ends

'When the thousand years are over, satan will be released from his prison and will go out to deceive the nations in the four corners of the earth – Gog and Magog – to gather them for battle. In number they are like the sand on the seashore. They marched across the breadth of the earth and surround the camp of God's people, the city he loves. But fire came from heaven and devoured them.' Revelation 20:7-9

Compare the plague that destroys the enemies of the Lord (Messiah), when he comes, with the fire that comes down from heaven on the last day, and destroys those who are not children of Israel.

'This is the plague with which the Lord will strike all the nations that fought against Jerusalem: Their flesh will rot while they are still standing on their feet, their eyes will rot in their sockets, and their tongues will rot

in their mouths. On that day men will be stricken by the Lord with great panic. Each man will seize the hand of another, and they will attack each other.' Zechariah 14:12-13

The crux of the problem is: we have preconceived ideas about the last days, and the purpose of the second coming of the Lord, which causes all sorts of problems in our understanding of what the scriptures have to say about the last days.

Why does He come the second time?
'For Christ did not enter a man-made sanctuary that was only a copy of the true one; he entered heaven itself, now to appear for us in God's presence. Nor did he enter heaven to offer himself again and again, the way the high priest enters the Most Holy Place every year with the blood that is not his own. Then Christ would have to suffer many times since the creation of the world. But now he has appeared once for all at the end of the ages to do away with sin by the sacrifice of himself. Just as man is destined to die once, and after that to face judgement, so Christ was sacrificed once to take away the sins of many people: and he will appear a second time, not to bear sin, but to bring salvation to those who are waiting.' Hebrews 9:24-28

It is obvious: neither Christians, nor Gentiles who refuse to repent, are waiting for salvation; but the Jews are. They wait for the coming of Messiah, their Kinsman Redeemer, to complete their salvation; for like the men of faith of the Old Testament, they have not received what was promised: Under the law they would not know the pardon, certainty and peace that Christians have.

'These were all commended for their faith, yet none of them received what was promised. God had planned something better for us so that only together with us would they be made perfect.' Hebrews 11:39-40

We can say with all assurance that the verses we are considering cannot refer to the Lord's second coming, but to the coming of The Lord

God Almighty the judge of all the earth. Therefore there is no need for any Christian to be alive when Messiah comes to bring salvation to the remnant of Israel.

The Kingdom is handed over
'We believe that Jesus died and rose again and so we believe that God will bring with Jesus those who have fallen asleep in Him.' 1 Thessalonians 4:14

'Then the end will come, when he (Jesus) hands over the kingdom to God the Father after he has destroyed all dominion, authority and power.' 1 Corinthians 15:24

The Ancient of Days - The Judge of all the Earth
'As I looked thrones were set in place, and the Ancient of days took his seat. His clothing was as white as snow; the hair of his head was white like wool. His throne was flaming with fire, and its wheels were all ablaze. A river of fire was flowing, coming out from before him. Thousands upon thousands attended him; ten thousand times ten thousand stood before him. The court was seated, and the books were opened.' Daniel 7:9-10

The Triune God, the Lord God Almighty, King of kings and Lord of lords, comes to judge the earth
'Then I saw a great white throne and Him who was seated on it. Earth and sky fled from His presence, and there was no place for them. And I saw the dead, great and small, standing before the throne, and books were opened. Another book was opened, which is the book of life. The dead were judged according to what they had done as recorded in the books. The sea gave up the dead that were in it, and death and Hades gave up the dead that were in them, and each person was judged according to what he had done. Then death and Hades were thrown into the lake of fire. The lake of fire is the second death. If anyone's name was not found written in the book of life, he was thrown into the lake of fire.' Revelation 20:11-12

There is much more that could be added, but I believe this is sufficient to show that this passage of scripture refers to the last day, the day of judgement, and the coming of the judge of all the earth; the Lord God Almighty, the triune God of Israel. Paul, I believe, is responding in these verses (1 Thessalonians 4:13-18) to questions that occurred to the Jews after Paul left them; perhaps after the three days of reasoning he had with them. (Acts 17:1-4) Paul would have told them that the elect gathered from the four winds of heaven, when Messiah returns, would be raised as souls, as spirits, from the first death until the day of the second resurrection; when they would be raised to life, body and soul. The second death would have no power over them.

John first of all saw their souls; then they came to life, body and soul.

'I saw thrones on which were seated those who had been given authority to judge. And I saw the souls of those who had been beheaded because of their testimony for Jesus and because of the word of God. They had not worshipped the beast or his image and had not received his mark on their foreheads or their hands. They came to life and reigned with Christ a thousand years. (The rest of the dead did not come to life until the thousand years were ended.) This is the first resurrection. Blessed and holy are those who have part in the first resurrection. The second death has no power over them, but they will be priests of God and of Christ and will reign with him for a thousand years.' Revelation 20:4-6

In his response, Paul includes all who have died in the Lord. The elect are gathered from the four winds of heaven; their souls raised from the first death at His second coming, now made alive, body and soul, at the second resurrection, when the 1,000 years end. The Jews who died during Christ's earthly reign who would not have been raised spiritually from the first death are also raised body and soul; then those who are alive and are left at his coming. All these are resurrected for judgement.

Are these the questions Paul is responding to?

"Paul, if the souls of the elect are raised from the first death when Messiah comes, what about our brothers who die during the thousand years of Messiahs reign? Their souls will not have been raised. And what about those who are alive, who are left on the last day, what happens to them? They will not be raised from the first death. Are they not also God's chosen people, His inheritance?"

Paul replies
'Brothers we do not want you to be ignorant about those who fall asleep'
1 Thessalonians 4:13-18

Contact the author by emailing to
Hugh.L.Mcknight@outlook.com

INSPIRED TO WRITE A BOOK?

Contact

Maurice Wylie Media
Inspirational Christian Publisher

Based in Northern Ireland and distributing around the world.
www.MauriceWylieMedia.com

The Table of Events

The Table of Events gives an overview of the Revelation as it unfolds. It is understood by reading across the page from column to column, with events on the same line, as one of the seal events, are referred to as parallel events in the study. When a seal event occurs, it is followed by one or more events of the sequence until the next seal event comes in the sequence. That in turn is followed by other events, and so on. These other events come in order, line by line, as we proceed down the table, showing in one or more of the columns the next event or events to take place in the revelation.

A parallel event is the same event given to us from two or more different sources, one of which must be a seal event. (Rev. 6) The other sources are: The Seven Trumpets (Rev. 8); the Seven Bowls of God's wrath (Rev.16) or from Daniel 11, The King of the South and the King of the North. They establish the order of events relative to one another, and confirm the chronological relationship of Daniel 11 to the unfolding Revelation.

The Seven Seals	Kings and Wars	Seven Trumpets and Seven Bowls of Wrath	The Three Woes	Acts of God and Heavenly Events
1st Seal				
A white horse-rider given a crown, held a bow-rode out to conquer. **Rev 6:2**	King of Persia invades countries north, south and west-no one could stop him. **Dan 11:2**	**1st Trumpet** Destructive weather – a third of the earth's trees and grass burned up. **Rev 8:7**		Feast of Weeks begins and 144,000 Jews sealed by God. **Rev 7:1-8**
2nd Seal				
A red horse-rider given power to take peace from the earth, given a large sword and power to make men slay one another. **Rev 6:3-4**	A mighty king rules with great power, takes peace from the earth. His kingdom divided into four **Dan 11:3**	**2nd Trumpet** A huge mountain all ablaze thrown into the sea. A third of all living creatures in the sea die. A third of ships destroyed. **Rev 8:8-9**		
	Diplomacy fails between the north and the south, Coup d'etat in the south. **Dan 11:6-7**	**3rd Trumpet** A great star blazing like a torch, fell from the sky on a third of the rivers and springs of waters. Many people died from the bitter waters. The name of the star is wormwood. **Rev 8:10-11**		
	King of south invades the north – wins. Leaves the north alone for a few years. King of the north invades the south - retreats and assembles a great army which will sweep on like a flood – as far as the fortress of the south. The king of the south fights the king of the north – wins and slaughters thousands. **Dan 11:7-12**	**4th Trumpet** A third of the sun - moon and stars was struck - they turned dark - a third of the day and night were without light. **Rev 8:12** **5th Trumpet** Demons released by satan from the Abyss - caused sores on those who did not have the seal of God – men long to die but death eludes them. (1st Woe) **Rev 9:1-12**	**1st Woe** The first woe is past; two other woes are yet to come. **Rev 9:12**	
	Northern king raises a huge army - south powerless to resist. King of the north establishes himself in the beautiful land - turns his attention to the coast lands - goes back to his own country - seen no more - kingdom divided into four. **Dan 11:13-19**	**6th Trumpet** Army of 200 million soldiers kill a third of mankind. **Rev 9:13-19**		
3rd Seal				
A black horse - rider holding a pair of scales given authority to rule - a litre of wheat - three litres of barley for a days wage. **Rev 6:5-6**	Tax-collector king - representative of the four northern kings - after a few years comes to his end. **Dan 11:20**			The angel and the little scroll. The mystery of God, revealed to the prophets, will be accomplished. **Rev 10:1-11**
			2nd Woe God's two witnesses appear, they witness for 1,260 days. **Rev 11:1-6**	
4th Seal		**7th Trumpet**		
A pale horse -rider named Death - Hades close behind - given power over a fourth of the earth to kill by sword and famine. **Rev 6:7-8**	Contemptible man comes to power - defeats three kings - unites the north - invades the south. **Dan 11:21-24**	Beast out of the sea and the beast out of the earth. **Rev 13:1-18**	**3rd Woe Begins** The king of the north given satanic power. **Rev 13:2**	The last week of years of the Feast of Weeks begins. **Dan 9:25-27** Heavenly affirmation of Israel's place in God's plan of redemption. **Rev. 12:1- 17**

The Seven Seals	Kings and Wars	Seven Trumpets and Seven Bowls of Wrath	The Three Woes	Acts of God and Heavenly Events
4st Seal (Continued)				
	The king of the south raises a large army but is defeated The two kings sit at the same table and lie to each other. The king of the north returns to his own country with great wealth - takes action against the holy covenant. **Dan 11:25-28**			144,000 first fruits, appear on mount Zion with the Lord. **Rev 14:1-5** Feast of Ingathering begins 1st Angel proclaims the Gospel to the whole world. **Rev 14:6-7** 2nd Angel foretells the destruction of Babylon the Great. **Rev 14:8** 3rd Angel warns not to worship the beast or his image or receive his mark on the forehead or hand. **Rev 14:9-12**
5th Seal				
Souls under the altar in heaven - slain for God's word - told to wait a little longer until the number of their fellow servants are killed to complete their number. **Rev 6:9-11**	North army desecrates the temple - sets up the abomination that causes desolation - forces everyone to receive the mark of the beast - abolishes the daily sacrifice - the hosts of the saints handed over - many killed by the sword, burned or captured. The king of the north does what he pleases - exults and magnifies himself above every god - speaks against the God of heaven - captures other lands At the time of the end the king of the south engages the king of the north in battle - the king of the north with the help of a foreign god attacks many countries - sweeps through them like a flood. Invades the beautiful land - destroys many - makes camp between the seas at the holy mountain. **Dan 11:29-44**			Then I heard a voice from heaven "Blessed are they who die in the Lord from now on." **Rev 14:13** Rebellion against God **2 Thess 2:1-4** Holy Spirit taken out of the way. **2 Thess 2-7**
			3rd Woe satan's power to rule on earth comes to climax. **Rev 17:15-18**	*Feast of Ingathering ends* The harvest of the earth Christians put to death. **Rev 14:14-17**
			2nd Woe ends God's two witnesses killed **Rev 11:7-14**	
				The harvest of 'grapes' gathered for the wine press of God's wrath. **Rev 14:18-20**
		God's Wrath Begins: **1st Bowl** - Painful sores on those with the mark of the beast. **2nd Bowl** - Sea turned to blood and everything died. **3rd Bowl** - The rivers and springs of water turned to blood. **4th Bowl** - Sun given power to scorch people. **5th Bowl** - The throne of the beast plunged into darkness - men cursed God because of their pains and sores. **6th Bowl** - Euphrates river dried up to make way for the kings of the earth to gather at Armageddon. **Rev 16:2-12**		

The Seven Seals	Kings and Wars	Seven Trumpets and Seven Bowls of Wrath	The Three Woes	Acts of God and Heavenly Events
6th Seal				
A great earthquake - the sun turned black like sackcloth - the moon turned blood red - the stars in the sky receded like a scroll being rolled up - every mountain and island were removed from their place. **Rev 6:12-17**		7th **Bowl** - A great earthquake. None like it since man has been on earth. Cities of the nations collapsed - huge hailstones fell upon men - they cursed God because the hail was huge, hailstones fell upon men - they cursed God because the hail was so terrible. **Rev 16:17-21**		God remembered Babylon the Great and gave her the cup filled with the wine of His wrath. **Rev 16:19**
				Feast of Weeks ends.
7th Seal				
White horse whose rider is called Faithful and True - dressed in a robe dipped in blood, and his name is the Word of God. The armies of heaven are following Him. **Rev 19:11-14**	The King of kings - The Lord of Lords. **Rev 19:16**			Feast of Trumpets sound Elect gathered from one end of heaven to the other.
	Messiah comes to reign **Zec 14:2-9**		3rd **Woe Ends**	**Mat 25:30-31**
			satan captured **Rev 20:1-3**	*Day of Atonement* The house of David saved by God's Grace **Zec 12:9-10**
	Christ's thousand year reign on earth begins. **Rev 20:1-3**			Feast of Tabernacles begins.
				The first Resurrection Blessed and holy are they for the second death has no power over them. **Rev 20:4-6**
	The thousand year reign ends **Rev 20:7**			Feast of Tabernacles ends.
			satan released from prison – goes out to deceive the nations - Gog and Magog gathered for battle - fire came down from heaven and destroyed them. **Rev 20:7-9** satan thrown into the lake of fire **Rev 20:10**	
	Kingdom handed over to the Father Almighty Then the end will come when He (Jesus) hands over the kingdom to God the Father after He has destroyed all dominion authority and power. **1 Cor 15:24**			
	The Lord Almighty comes with a loud command with the trumpet call of God **1 Thess 4:16-17**			The second resurrection The dead in Christ are raised first. After that those who are still alive are caught up together with them in the clouds to meet the Lord in the air. **1 Thess 4:16-17** The day of judgement
	Then I saw a Great White Throne and Him who was seated on it. Earth and sky fled from His presence and there was no place for them. And I saw the dead, great and small, standing before the throne and books were opened. Another book was opened, which is the book of life The dead are judged by what they had done as recorded in the books. **Rev 20:11-12**	The sea gave up the dead that were in it, and death and Hades gave up the dead that were in them, and each person was judged according to what he had done. Then death and hades were thrown into the lake of fire. The lake of fire is the second death. If anyone's name was not found written in the book of life, he was thrown into the lake of fire. **Rev 20:13-15**		*Sabbath begins* Then I saw a new heaven and a new earth and the Holy City the new Jerusalem - Now the dwelling of God is with men, and He will live with them - and be their God. **Rev 21, 22**

9 781999 795597